PRAISE FOR CINELLE BARNES

Praise for *Malaya: Essays on Freedom*

"Cinelle Barnes steps into the full power of her voice with *Malaya*. In this collection of deftly woven and deeply resonant essays, Barnes intertwines past and present as she reflects on the daily realities of those who are undocumented, the healing powers of dance and memoir, and the fears and joys of raising a brown daughter in a country in denial about the depths of its own racism. Told in sharp, luminous prose, *Malaya* reminds us of how vital this (re)birthing process we call writing truly is. With compassion and conviction, Barnes bears witness to stories that so often go untold—and asserts the possibility of a world where those we love have the freedom to tell their own."

—Zeyn Joukhadar, author of *The Map of Salt and Stars*

"In *Malaya*, Cinelle Barnes asks the essential question: How do we free ourselves? Her essays explore what it means to live authentically as a woman, a person of color, an immigrant, a human being, not in the hands or eyes of others but in her own heart. Barnes tells her story with clarity and honesty and, in doing so, clears a path for the rest of us to follow."

—Victoria Loustalot, author of *Future Perfect: A Skeptic's Search for an Honest Mystic*, *Living like Audrey: Life Lessons from the Fairest Lady of All*, and *This Is How You Say Goodbye: A Daughter's Memoir*

"I'm sure many readers of *Malaya* will focus on words like strength, resolve, and pride, but I'm most taken by Barnes's radical deploying of surrender in these essays. The book is neither solipsistic nor rooted in brittle hope. Instead it's a textured meditation on how embodied acceptance and surrender are often the most radical of gestures when it comes to provocative art making."

—Kiese Laymon, author of *Heavy: An American Memoir, Long Division*, and *How to Slowly Kill Yourself and Others in America*

"'I write because I am the last to remember,' Cinelle Barnes tells us in her essay 'Why I Write Memoir.' *Malaya* is a sensitive, vibrant book that will help so many of us remember and reflect on the stories we shouldn't forget. Barnes's deft writing crosses gaps in time, understanding, and experience, illuminating important truths about our country and culture while also allowing us to bear witness to her own fight for healing, justice, and belonging. *Malaya* is a book we need, and Cinelle Barnes is a writer to treasure."

—Nicole Chung, author of *All You Can Ever Know*

Praise for *Monsoon Mansion: A Memoir*

"Reminiscent of both Jeanette Walls's memoir, *The Glass Castle* (2005), and Sandra Cisneros's seminal novel *The House on Mango Street* (1984), this is a story of a tragic childhood told in a remarkably uplifting voice. Barnes imbues scenes from her interrupted childhood with an artistic touch that reads like literary fiction. Luminescent and shattering, Barnes's first book is a triumph: a conquering of the past through the power of the written word."

—*Booklist* (starred review)

"We implore you to get your hands on this harrowing and triumphant coming-of-age story set in the Philippines."

—*Hyphen Magazine*

"Through the course of Barnes's work, we come to find that the body does have mechanisms for survival and that sometimes the twinning of resolve and perseverance can lead to small moments of grace."

—*The Margins*

"Stuck in a tangled web of betrayal, Barnes's harrowing coming-of-age memoir reveals the strength we don't know we have until we are forced to use it."

—*She Reads*

"Cinelle Barnes's debut memoir is filled with the joy and pain of childhood. Set strikingly against the backdrop of Mansion Royale and the rich Philippine landscape, Barnes weaves the complex story of her family and the shifting dynamics that rocked her childhood. This memoir—a fairy tale turned survival story—strikes at the heart of what it means to grow up and face the reality of family."

—Culture Trip

"In this gut-wrenching riches-to-rags story, author Cinelle Barnes recounts growing up in the shadow of her family's fall from grace in the Philippines, and what exactly it took to survive . . . Beautiful prose [and] evocative detail . . . make the pages of *Monsoon Mansion* fly."

—*Bustle*

"Barnes hopes that *Monsoon Mansion* will provide some comfort to other survivors of childhood trauma. But she also hopes that the book builds empathy in people who don't have experience with abuse, poverty, or war."

—*Bustle*

"If you enjoy memoirs that take you to a life, location, and world entirely different from your own, bump *Monsoon Mansion* to the top of your TBR list."

—*Hello Giggles*

"A young essayist's memoir of her extraordinary riches-to-rags childhood in the Philippines . . . In this tender and eloquent tale, the author plumbs the depths of family dysfunction while telling a harrowing story of survival graced by moments of unexpected magic. A lyrically heartfelt memoir of resilience in the face of significant obstacles."

—*Kirkus Reviews*

"Barnes's aptly titled debut memoir, *Monsoon Mansion*, is saturated in pain, trauma, and, at times, pure joy. This is Barnes's childhood in the Philippines—one she describes as both mesmerizing and horrifying."

—*Charleston City Paper*

"In this incandescent debut memoir, Cinelle Barnes forges memories of her family's downfall with tumultuous Filipino history. Like the storm in its title, *Monsoon Mansion* immerses us in the darkest waters of memory, stirring up unbearably brutal childhood events with lyrical prose and searing imagery, forming a woven tale that is both delicate and electric. This book assures us that even when we lose those things that give shape to our humanity—our roots, culture, and family—we can go on to devise a new way of being."

—Susan Tekulve, author of *In the Garden of Stone*

"The princess becomes a pauper before she turns eleven, yet through grit and love and words, that princess, Cinelle Barnes, escapes a fallen-in mansion and broken family to survive. Light fills this beautiful memoir—breaking through the dark loneliness of a mansion with no electricity. And light will fill you and carry you on, dear reader, even after you turn the last page. *Monsoon Mansion* sings a song of rain and sparkling light, and like its author, we'll all come to know the diamonds we carry in our palms."

—Jim Minick, author of *Fire Is Your Water*

"*Monsoon Mansion* is a classic memoir that will reach every part of the world today with its personal story of love, heartbreak, betrayal, belief, and survival. An unforgettable tale of our time."

—Dan Wakefield, author of *Going All the Way* and *New York in the Fifties*

"Writing about young warrior girls is my forte, so believe me when I tell you that Cinelle's strength, the one that carried her through years of darkness to then relive them in the forging of these pages, is dazzling. Blindingly so. Her prose sears. Her story illuminates. Every memory in *Monsoon Mansion* burns, but there's healing in the flames, somehow, because Cinelle stands on the other side of the inferno—shining."

—Ryan Graudin, author of *Wolf by Wolf*

MALAYA

ALSO BY CINELLE BARNES

Monsoon Mansion: A Memoir

MALAYA

ESSAYS ON FREEDOM

CINELLE
BARNES

Published by Little A, New York

www.apub.com

Amazon, the Amazon logo, and Little A are trademarks of Amazon.com, Inc., or its affiliates.

ISBN-13: 9781542093309 (hardcover)
ISBN-10: 1542093309 (hardcover)

ISBN-13: 9781542093323 (paperback)
ISBN-10: 1542093325 (paperback)

Cover design by Faceout Studio, Lindy Martin

Cover illustration by Monica Ramos

Printed in the United States of America

First edition

For my daughter
For the fight

We cannot talk about our oppressors without talking about those whom we oppress.

—Hala Alyan

Contents

INTRODUCTION

MALAYA

It was in a Greek art history class at Hunter College in New York City that I first heard about the Pythia and her duties as an oracle. My professor was an Italian American archaeologist who'd traveled to Samothrace, a small Greek island in the Aegean Sea, and brought twenty or so projector slides to class that night, though she showed us only four and spent almost three hours talking about a cup from the fifth century BC. An unknown artist had painted the cup's surface with a female figure on the left and a male figure on the right. The female sat on a tall tripod, which looked to me like a barstool, and the male stood across from her, his eyes set on her face. Her eyes avoided his stare as she looked, chin to chest, into the hollow of the wide-brimmed, shallow bowl in her hand. There was a floor beneath them, depicted as a bold line, and there was a ceiling, too. But most notable to me at the time was the pillar between them: a *physical* separation that could be penetrated by his gaze, and, I assumed from his stance and gesture, his want. I'd seen this look before, this penetrating scrutiny.

The female figure was the Pythia, Apollo's oracle. The night I learned about her, I learned that her story was my own. When I saw the oracle sitting on her stool, I saw myself: a girl sitting on a meter-high stack of secrets, of predictions that kept her separate from the people her prose and poetry, energy and ecstasy, analyses and intuition, faith and fidelity were meant to serve. I caught a few phrases the professor threw in the air: *The oracle was separated in a temple, free from association and contact. They consulted her because she was removed from their day-to-day. She had the perspective of an outsider. Young, innocent.*

I was an undocumented immigrant, shuttled and shipped from the Philippines as an unaccompanied minor, adopted into a new family and a new country. I was young, with a complexion that was "enviably tan" but also "too dark," and physically, emotionally, and culturally separated from my mother and father. I had an affinity for poetry and prose that dated back to primary school, and I had an ecstatic, erratic, storied, historied spiritual life. I knew ritual—I had worked as a cleaning lady, and I had performed as a dancer. And, like clergy, I was a frequent recipient of people's inquiries and stories.

What should I do? they often asked, and I returned counsel in exchange for space in their insular White worlds. An unspoken transaction: you give me a seat at your dinner table, I give you opinions or advice.

On life decisions:

Should I quit my job and go back to school?

Should I quit my job and travel to Southeast Asia?

Should I tell my mother I'm quitting?

On things they already knew:

Is it abuse if he doesn't let me own a smartphone?

Is it abuse if he doesn't let me see my friends?

Is it abuse if they walked around naked, day and night, even though they never touched me?

Things I wish *I* could write—people are such great writers when they tell the truth:

When he told me why he wanted to die, all I could think of was the custard bubbling out of the pie and that I needed to take the pie out of the oven.

I couldn't call it rape because he had dementia. People with dementia sleepwalk, and sometimes they sleepwalk into your bed.

Between babysitting and waiting tables, I read up on the oracle on the subway. It was before I had a smartphone, and I read from textbooks with pages that felt like cellophane. I had already developed a habit of dog-earing; the books weren't mine but the sentences belonged to me. When the authors described the Pythia's ceremonial activities, her invisibility most days and hypervisibility during scheduled rites, the questions the men of the polis asked, the eloquence with which she suggested that a war either commence or stop, I thought of how I, too, had been selected without having a choice. I, too, had certain ceremonies to follow, lest I get caught and deported. I, too, had been both invisible and hypervisible with such intermittence that I could appear as frantic, frenzied. Like her, I've had to answer people and answer *to* people—mostly men (though women are also culpable), mostly White, mostly with some kind of power: at school, at work, at the USCIS office, at urgent care, in romantic relationships. I've had to give them my words to secure our friendship and, therefore, my safety.

And I have had a relationship with language for as long as I can remember. I dog-eared a nursery rhyme at age three so I could have my brother read it to me daily. I wrote my first poem at age six and my first story at seven. Truly, though, a relationship with *languages*—English, Tagalog, and Spanish—is what I have. I know to code switch depending on who I'm talking to or what about. Like the ancient oracle, I live in the liminal and translate from mysteries: the enigma of another culture, of color, of being born female. Everyday people love me, so I tell them things. But they are also unsure of me, so I only tell them some.

I don't tell them that I fled from a home built on ill-gotten wealth and from a mother and stepfather who withheld food and water and killed my pet chicken. I don't tell them that I sneaked into this country with one duffel bag and one pair of shoes on a plane from Manila to Honolulu, from Honolulu to San Francisco. I don't tell them that a USCIS officer told me, as he passed my rejected forms across the metal table, *I'm sorry, kid. I'm so sorry. You have to leave.* And I don't tell them that when he said this, he cleared his throat, shook his head, winked, and mouthed, *Stay*, as he brought his index finger to his pursed lips. It was the first of many secrets I was to keep.

I don't tell anybody that I am still confused about why or how he winked at me, whether it was the way my birth father winked at me after finding me hiding in a bookstore, or the way my stepfather winked at me before he hurt my mother. I don't tell anybody—not even people of color—that before I was an author, I was a cleaning lady, a laundromat worker, a nanny. Before the bachelor's degree in journalism and art history and the MFA in creative writing, I had to take the Test of English as a Foreign Language to prove to an American high school that I could speak English. As if they didn't know or didn't remember that the Philippines was colonized by the Americans after the Spanish left, that we adopted English as a trade and instructional language, or that many 1-800 calls are received not in the United States, but in some cubicle in Manila, Cebu, or Davao. No one saw the irony when I began to tutor my American-born counterparts in US history.

I don't tell anyone that I hate pickles, white bread, and coleslaw, and that I love to eat chicken feet and octopus. I suck the juices from the bone or tentacle, and I let them drip from my chin because that's what island people do.

The oracle was separated in a temple, free from association and contact. They consulted her because she was removed from their day-to-day.

In 2018, over a decade after I met the Pythia in art history class, I published *Monsoon Mansion*, a memoir about the traumatic childhood

I had survived. Well received in that it garnered a vast readership and positive notes from reviewers and the media, the book, hence or however, opened a time in my life when I'd be put on what was like a tripod stool—to be examined, to answer so many questions, to reach into and feel so many wounds, and to defend my narrative and justify the telling of it when, it seemed, my written words did not do enough to pet someone's ego. A majority of the audience was receptive and warm—some even sent gift cards for Filipino baked goods or paid for my post-book-event meals—but still, when anyone asked at a reading or a signing or online, *What will you write next?* I was afraid to tell them the truth.

When I don't know what to write, or when I hesitate to write, I go back to the oracle in my dreams. I consult her, and she shows me the contents of her shallow bowl. There aren't any dice, lots, or laurel sprigs. But there is a piece of paper in my handwriting: lines of cursive *O*s, line after line after line. Each *O* is an oval in black ink, the kind of black that inks out of my favorite fine-tipped pen. Calligraphy is something I've taken with me across oceans: the twist of the tilde, the sharp tips of the hard *K* and the cross of the *t*, the curves of double vowels. They are symbols for sounds, sounds that may not be audible here, in America, in the temple. In my dreams, I take the oracle's hand and lead her away from her uneasy perch. We break down the pillar. We have told them some, but we have omitted so much. I keep leading her away from the stool, and I tell her that she no longer needs to tell them what they want to hear. We step out of the temple together, and I give us a new name: *Malaya*, which in my language means "to be free." She hands me a pen and paper. I take it. I begin.

And here are the stories of my pursuits—yes, plural—of freedom. Here is what I've been wanting to tell them, to tell you. Here, too, I describe not only those who have oppressed me or those like me, but also those I have enabled, those I have propped up, those I have stepped on. If I am going to try to write about freedom, especially at such a time, I must be comprehensive. I must tell myself things, too.

Yours

1

I am a teenage girl holding a baby outside the Manila airport, and two strangers are approaching me. One of them reaches for the baby, and the other hands me a brown envelope. I don't take it. It's early enough in the evening that there is plenty of noise from the street to swallow the sound of my pleading. I am clutching the baby, refusing to give him away. The two women shake their heads as they draw in closer, and one reveals the contents of the brown envelope: a passport and a sheet of paper. The writing on the paper makes me surrender the baby, who is old enough to hold his head up and old enough to know when he is being held by a stranger. He cries. I do, too. I turn away and walk up to the revolving door, and as it spins, it throws back images of the baby being bounced, shushed, and taken away. The door keeps turning, like a flip-book, and the images turn with it; smaller and smaller they get, and softer the cries become, until the baby is gone. I step in, and I am on the other side.

2

You were eight when you told me you wanted to become an artist and asked me to teach you how to draw a dog. So I drew an upside-down heart and accented it with whiskers, and drew a *U* for the tongue, a dotted circle for the face, and bell-shaped ears. You followed each step, and your dog turned out to be more realistic than mine—better. This was how I knew you'd be okay. That should I leave again, you'd find me and you'd find yourself. That you understood home was your drawing and painting; home was my writing and reading. Home is the imagination.

3

I am no longer in Manila, but at a kitchen table in the suburbs of Long Island. I am chewing my corned beef and soda bread with no sound, careful not to let broth squish through one side of my mouth, careful not to drop bread crumbs on the tartan tablecloth. Before the women took the baby, before the revolving door, I was a talker. Once I got in trouble with the nuns at my school for telling a joke during mass. Now I only say *more please* and *thank you*, and *good night* when my new mother pulls the door closed and heads downstairs, when all I can hear are my sniffles and the hiss of the radiator. I am not sure if I am crying because there is a need for a radiator—it snows from before until after Christmas where my adoptive family lives. I am not sure if I am crying because tomorrow is a school day and I will be eating lunch alone again, at the library, chewing with no sound. But I am certain that at least part of the crying is because I don't know where you are. I don't know if someone bought you a cake when you turned one, or if someone adopted you like someone adopted me, and if you've had to adjust to your new family's rules and routine, their collective personality. My new family is quiet, and so I have become quiet. And the quiet makes it easier to hear what lingers from the night you were taken.

4

The first time someone was taken from my family was in 1954, just a decade after the Philippines helped the United States defeat Japan. My grandfather had a stall at the wet market, and my grandmother was working as a seamstress. Together they ran a tailoring shop, but they had nine children, and so three jobs weren't enough. There was no way my grandmother could take on more work, as she had the responsibility of rearing children, and the only way to survive was not to take on more but to give away. When Manay, a wealthy distant relative, came over for pan de coco and Coca-Cola one afternoon, the relative was happy to see my grandmother but annoyed at the flies hovering over the plate of pan, annoyed at the intermittence of young ones crawling or toddling up to my grandmother, and annoyed at how hot it was—that my grandparents could not afford an air conditioner. It was post–World War II, the American era. It did not make sense to Manay how someone during such a time could still not afford advancements introduced to us by the same people who brought us Levi's and John Wayne. She said, *I know! I'll take one of the children back with me for a night to relieve you some.* Manay took the third youngest—young enough to cuddle, old enough to use the bathroom on his own. And since he walked up to the plate of pan de coco more than the others did, she thought that he would enjoy her restaurant. She lived on the other side of Panay island—two jeepneys and a tricycle transfer away—so he was famished by the time they got to the restaurant, an annex to her air-conditioned house. He ate platefuls that night and the morning after.

5

Do you remember that June afternoon I left New York to live closer to the man I was marrying? Do you remember running after me as I lugged my suitcase down the driveway and to the cab? You were not yet a teenager, not yet as old as I was the first time I became part of a familial transaction in America, our adopted country. Why was this our fate, you seemed to ask, when you wrapped both arms around me, blubbering into my side, sopping my dress with your tears. I wanted to tell you then that this was part of the deal—this was how the business of moving in or up in this country, at least for newcomers like us, was conducted. For every leg up or hand out, something had to be given up: proximity to our culture, to the kind of food we were accustomed to eating, to the language we spoke and dreamt in, to kin. But I loved this man and he loved me, I told you, so this was the best kind of transaction of all. I would visit and you could visit, I assured you. But I never promised that this would be the last time you would hurt this way.

6

I am so quiet that even my new quiet family is alarmed. Years later, I will come across "Daughter," a poem by James Lenfestey. The poem's narrator says that their daughter is not like a passing cloud, but a permanent one, and she hangs and casts a shadow over the earth. She sleeps in her upstairs room, is silent and mysterious, and blows cold and warm air down the steps. I will think, *Is this what I did to the person who brought me to America, when all she wanted to do was to save me from the tragedy back home?*

7

Manay did not return the boy to my grandmother on the second day nor the third. On the fourth day, with four kids in tow, she took two jeepneys and a tricycle to the other side of the island to look for her son. They arrived at dinnertime, when the restaurant was at its busiest, and from the front window looked for the boy. My father, then around nine years old, stood on a rickety bench to get a better view. He cupped his hands around his face as he peered in, blocking out the glare from the setting sun. And on the far side of the restaurant, the side where the counter was set up and the steaming plates of food were coming out of the kitchen, he saw my chubby young uncle smiling and sitting on a barstool, hunched over a tray of rice, noodle soup, fritters, and cola with crushed ice. My grandmother saw him, too. And when she did, she hoisted the littlest to her hip and told the others to follow as she walked back toward the tricycle stand. That was the last thing she said until they got home and she needed to tell them that it was time for their bath.

8

I told my husband, the one I left New York—you—for, that he needed to sit down for the news I was about to share. My brother might go to prison. But that wasn't the news. The news was that my brother—your father—needed our help in a specific, familiar kind of way.

9

My adoptive mother, a middle-aged widow who lives in one of the wealthiest towns on Long Island, can buy me anything. She buys Nutri-Grain bars when I grow wide-eyed watching a commercial for the gooey snack. She buys a silver-and-blue CD player when she hears me hum a song in the back seat of the Lexus. She buys a Ralph Lauren fleece jacket when she sees that this is the brand and style the high school kids wear. And for my seventeenth birthday, she buys a white dress with a handkerchief hem from Lord & Taylor, one she hopes I will wear not only on my biological birthday—the day I was born—but also on my new birthday, or the day I will officially be adopted, naturalized, Americanized.

10

I was in New York on business, to meet with my literary agent. Your father was texting me during the meeting, incessantly, and my phone flashed green so often that I had to turn it facedown. I NEED TO ASK YOU SOMETHING. CALL PLS. He knew I was in the city for a few days, strictly for work and on a tight schedule. I had a hunch it was about you—they always asked *me* about you: Why does he spend so much time in his room? Why does he draw all day? Where does his mind go when he stares out the window, or when he sits in that old swing? They believed I could read people—that I could read you. But no. That was not the inquiry at all. Your father sat across from me at the Starbucks outside Penn Station, fidgeting with a plastic straw, avoiding my eyes. He told me that when he left the job at the flower farm and got the job at the tech school, he might have agreed to assist in "less than legal" operations. He said yes because fifteen dollars per hour was better than eight dollars per hour, and he had four mouths to feed. Transactions, love—don't they mean the same? He mentioned going to jail or getting sent back home, said he didn't know what to do, and I said, with only half a breath between his confession and my reaction, *I will take care of it. I will adopt him.*

11

According to my father, Manay never officially adopted his chubby little brother. But what was official then? Just fifty-six years prior, in 1898, Spain surrendered the Philippines to the United States for $20 million under the Treaty of Paris. Does the financial transaction make the Philippines property or an adoptee? Do the platefuls of fritters and bottles of ice-cold Coca-Cola make my uncle property or an adoptee? Was he an immigrant within his own clan, a chubby child whose work was to keep the restaurant atmosphere lively, to gobble up food excitedly and entertain customers, in exchange for his stay at the air-conditioned house? Was it a transaction if there was love?

12

But I loved this man and he loved me, I told you, so this was the best kind of transaction of all.

13

I thought I had unofficially adopted you when I was sixteen; when they all left for America for a better life; when I held you in the van that took us to the airport; when, at first, I refused to give you to those women; when I decided to finally relinquish you because it meant me on a plane to New York, where I hoped to find your parents and siblings, where I hoped to one day send you toys and money from, where I hoped we would be reunited.

14

The widow looks forward to the day when she will officially become my mother. *Would you like to call me Mother?* I look down at my feet. *Auntie is fine, just fine.*

She *is* Auntie—my father's oldest sister. We'd never met before the corned beef and soda bread, the Nutri-Grain bars, the CD player, or the handkerchief hem, but the widow has heard some about my misfortunes back home. She has heard about my mentally ill and negligent mother, my abusive stepfather, and my father's refusal to stay put and build a home. She flew me to the United States because I had nowhere to go, had nobody to care for me, and there was now an empty room upstairs. Newly widowed, almost empty nested, with much love to give.

15

Is it bad that I daydream about my brother going to prison? I want, with the kind of urgency I labored and pushed my daughter with, to make you a part of our family. I want to set up an easel on the balcony for you. I want to enroll us in surf lessons. I want to take you and your now cousin, soon-to-be sister to the beach on Sundays. I want to teach you how to make chicken marsala and pumpkin muffins. I want to show you how to be a good, great immigrant and tell you how I made it from quiet adopted child to star student to author. I want to help you navigate the in-betweens of child, student, and author. I want to because I believe I am the best for you. (This is what all prospective parents say at their screening interviews.) The best then, the best now. Because I have lived your life.

16

INA 101(b)(1)(E) permits a US citizen to petition for a child who was adopted while under the age of sixteen, and has been in the legal custody of, and has resided with, the adopting parent or parents for at least two years.

This is what the immigration officer reads from his clipboard on the day of my supposed new birthday. I am wearing the white dress and using the handkerchief hem to wipe the corners of my eyes when the officer breaks the news: *I'm sorry, kid. I'm so sorry. You have to leave.* Does the widow know this? Did she not consult her lawyer about this? Was she aware that I was too old to become an American through adoption? Is this why she bought the dress that doubles as a hanky? Did she expect tears? Did she expect a miracle?

17

Here's a miracle:

I am playing with my nephew, the baby separated from me at the airport, and he is now two years old and has four front teeth. We are in a backyard in Long Island that has a thrift-store swing. He is strapped in and smiling, swinging back and forth, his fingers curled around the ropes connecting the Little Tikes seat and the tree branch. I am pushing him, higher and higher, whoosh, and telling him to reach up for the low-hanging leaves. We do this every day around ten, after his morning snack, and again at five thirty, just before his mom and dad return from working at a flower farm. Working at the farm allowed them to save money for the baby's passport, visa, and plane ticket. And my falling out of adoption and citizenship—my lack of papers, my out-of-status—allows them to work now that they have the baby back. Sometimes things work out. Milagro.

18

The baby girl I pushed into a birthing pool is now six, and she is much like you. She likes to draw, to paint, to read to the potted plants on the porch, to stay in her room, to be quiet. She is much like you, which means she is much like me. Words, images—where we three live. Home is, even here and even now, in the imagination.

She wrote a poem and read it to me last night: fish live in water / ideas live in my brain / books live in the library / my bed lives in a house / you live in my heart / I love you

But sometimes I wonder if she imagines things the way you and I imagine them. She is half-White, after all. Born here, she has never known the threat of getting deported, has never been left behind, taken, given. These are the things I prayed she wouldn't have to endure, but these are also the things that keep me from knowing what it's like to be her.

I want to because I believe I am the best for you. (This is what all prospective parents say at their screening interviews.) The best then, the best now. Because I have lived your life.

I am certain that I am the best for you. But for her?

19

My father admitted to me that he envied his brother. His brother never had to shine shoes, haul vegetable crates, or sell peanuts outside the movie theater. His brother never had to sleep on cardboard and wake up to prickly heat on his neck and back. My father also admitted to me that he never wanted such a life for his own children—which is why he left for Saudi Arabia, for Taiwan, Japan, Malaysia, Australia. He was the breadwinner turned absentee father. Our country is a country of breadwinners turned absentee mothers and fathers. We measure our gross domestic product by the number of fathers and mothers that leave: two million in 2016.

What we don't measure: How many millions of children are left behind?

20

You visited the summer before you turned sixteen—the last summer you were, according to immigration law, eligible for naturalization through adoption. We learned to surf, and, similar to drawing, you were better at it than I was. You could pop up to your feet, while I could barely stay on the board lying on my stomach. You caught waves and rode them, and welcomed each spray from the ocean with your mouth wide open, never blinking, unaware that your legal status in the United States was like riding that board—you could fall off. Your father hadn't told you he was on trial and could go to prison. I hadn't told you I was preparing to adopt you; that I had downloaded, printed, and signed the paperwork; or that I had thought about the color scheme for your room. And the government hadn't told us if they were keeping the DREAM Act or not.

I watched the ocean. Curl or no curl? Choppy or flat? Was it coming up to a swell? Was it moving to barrel you in?

I watched you. You nodded at the surf instructor, repeated what he said. He was telling you about duck diving, that sometimes you have to push the board nose-first into the water, not riding over the wave, but under.

21

Your father did not go to prison. YOUR FATHER DID NOT GO TO PRISON. Milagro, the family said. Sometimes things work out. Milagro. Everyone was certain they would find him guilty. Everyone was certain he would get sent to jail or, at the very least, sent back home. But all they gave him was community service. All they wanted was his cooperation, some information. All I wanted was you.

22

What has become of me? How did I go from girl with a baby at the airport, to girl who blows leaves down the stairs, then cold air, then warm, to woman who wishes her brother imprisoned? Nobody deserves a child who stops talking. Nobody deserves my ill will upon them. Nobody deserves to lose their child just so another could have someone to hold, to love. When people adopt, when does it stop being about the child and when does it start being about the grown-up? *I believe I am the best for you. (This is what all prospective parents say at their screening interviews.)* Perhaps I know when it started: when I was an orphan myself. Orphaned children are born complete but grow up believing something is missing. The circle begins not at the revolving door, but at the moment when my mother abandoned me for her hallucinations and my father abandoned me for his Third World dreams. And the circle ends before it is complete—you are not mine; this is not a full circle.

And yet this is another milagro. This is the ocean barreling in. On me, not you. This is me lying on the surfboard, unable to pop up, unable to keep from slipping. This is the water rising over me and pulling me under, nose-first, swirling me down until I hit a rock. It is the water—God, life—telling me what I need to be telling you: What is best for you is already yours—you.

To Care, to Care Too Much

I don't clean our house except when guests come, and even then, they sit just a breath away from having a tower of laundry or stacks of drafts fall on them. My inattentiveness in this part of domesticity bothers neither my husband nor my daughter, so why change? As long as my daughter has a swimsuit that is more pliable than brittle when she has swim-team practice, and as long as our plates and pans hold less-than-harmful traces of salmonella or the like, we can call ourselves a happy family.

I tell my two that this is happiness for me: not to care.

My first job in the United States was to clean houses with my biological siblings. Newly adopted but also newly undocumented at age seventeen, and poor, I cleaned houses on Long Island for six dollars per hour. I should have been getting ready to go to college, but my having fallen out of legal immigration status impeded my advancing and, for the first time since I learned how to read, I was uninterested in school. I suffered from acedia, from the Latin and Greek words that meant *negligence* or *lack of care*. Formerly a dancer, a soccer player (team captain), and an A student at an art honors high school program, I suddenly—and I mean *suddenly*—could not bring myself to do anything.

One afternoon, an immigration officer handed me rejected naturalization forms, and the next morning, my legs didn't know how to kick a ball and my penmanship went from Catholic-school approved to illegible. I went from being nearly ambidextrous to nondexterous, unable to shave my legs, brush my hair, type into my LiveJournal interface or AOL status, draw, or write. Family members who came to say they were sorry about the bad news would now likely describe this time as my having stayed in bed for days on end. But their definition does not fit the experience. I did not *stay* in bed. My more accurate description is that I *left*. I had fought for citizenship and a new life in America—that was the fight response to the trauma I experienced in the Philippines. And when that response didn't work, my spirit or gumption or essence departed from my body. I was, but not in the hyperbolic teenage sense, *so done*.

My biological sister, twenty years my senior, who took me in when I was twelve and again when my naturalization forms were denied and I left my adoptive parents' home, knew of only one way to cure me. She forced me to move my body. She said that I should clean houses with her and our brother, convinced that if I could hold a brush and get into the rhythm of scrubbing in an up-down-up-down motion, I could get better. I scrubbed grout on my first day. On my second day, my sister encouraged me to move on to windows, to circular hand movements, *Karate Kid*–style. This took weeks to master. This demanded both sides of the brain to work. This, then, awakened two sides of my being that had fallen dormant—the left and the right, or in what I would later learn as a young mother in therapy, narrative (explicit) memory and emotional (implicit) memory.

Grime lifted off the glass, and I felt some rigidity lift off my body. When I could press Windex-wet rags hard enough against glass to make it squeak, my sister put my right hand on a vacuum cleaner handle and my left hand around a vacuum cleaner cord. She turned it on and said, "Clean in rows." By then, my body could simultaneously hold the weight of the refurbished '90s-era machine and coordinate to make plaid patterns on the carpet. My body moved forth and back, which, if your body had just been told it could not have space in a country, doubled as an exercise in mobility, space-making, and space-holding.

My sister, who was already like a mother to me, intuitively acted as my physical therapist. Ever wary of talking about mental health, as most Filipinos her age were and still are, she committed herself to my functional recuperation. This was care, too, despite the lack of vocabulary and inclination necessary to tackle what was really a problem of the mind. My biological family believed problems of the mind were too expensive for us, too affluent, too White. We were new immigrants, thirteen of us split between two bedrooms, collecting ingredients for our meals from the discounted meat rack at Western Beef and the Asian grocery store, from the local food pantry, and from the near-expired or out-of-season stock they left at the truck loading port behind the CVS. We ate pumpkin-spice bread in the late winter and Easter candy in the summer. Once, we ate corn for two weeks straight because a local farmers market had garbage bags of cobs to throw away. My brother and I salvaged them, walking home with big bags of corn on our backs, like Santa bringing presents on Christmas Day. And it was like Christmas—my sister's and my brother's kids hoorayed when we dumped out a mound of yellow onto the kitchen floor.

This was our plight. We didn't know, or didn't feel permitted, or it felt extravagant and even dangerous—would they report us to immigration services?—to consult a licensed counselor on my condition.

How my sister fixed me is not how I would choose to help myself or someone else today, but it worked. A few months in, while I had completely abandoned sports, I could at least walk lengths that were four times as long as a soccer field. I regained speed, too. My legs remembered that I played midfield. I used my reclaimed speed to dust, scrub, sweep, and mop twice as fast as when I first started, leaving our team with more time to take on more jobs. Business was good. We got ourselves a brand-new, cordless, weightless, bright-orange vacuum cleaner from Walmart.

My brother, in charge of publicizing our services by word of mouth, kept booking jobs, and I kept showing up to work. It was regularity, or progression, or some sort of combination of both. We set up a small dry-erase board on our kitchen wall for writing our weekly schedule, and the check marks we drew in the columns after each job felt gratifying. Still, I did most of the work while crying silently so my sister wouldn't hear me while she folded clothes or changed linens in the next room. I cleaned mostly while sniffling, the sides of my nose becoming gray black from the dust or soot transferred from my hands. When I wiped tears with my shirt, I smelled the scent of the Fabuloso or Pine-Sol it had absorbed.

I was scrubbing the inside of a toilet when I started to sob and heave one morning. My back arched and my torso bent over the bowl, my hair falling toward the electric-blue Lysol water. I bawled with such force—as if my body was remembering it was animate, organic. My entire skin, my largest organ, felt wet, like a baby fresh from the sac. If dying is the driest our bodies could be, this was a waking up, a wetness that signaled life was coming—or, in my case, coming back. My sister heard what my body was doing in the bathroom, that I know, but she didn't come to my rescue or yell from where she was. She let me be with my body, let my body do what it had to do, which was learning to care again. She also didn't come, because that would have encouraged talking. Immigrants do. Immigrants don't talk.

Over a decade later, I would acquire the habit of telling myself or my husband or my daughter that when we show signs of anxiety such as nail-biting, fidgeting, stuttering, or hiding, that we are acting nervous because we care. There are these movements because there is thought.

And every time I say this, we feel less guilty for having bodies that move the way they do.

We didn't yet own a vehicle during our cleaning days, so my brother asked people to drive us to our jobs, along with our dollar-store caddies of cleaners, scrubbers, and rags. Often, whoever drove us to our "office for the day" (as we jokingly said) ended up mopping or dusting with us, earning not only gas money for the ride but money for their time. This person was usually a relative or a new friend from the local Filipino community who worked nights and weekends as a nursing assistant or home health aide, who had time to spare but turned that time into extra cash—remittances. When we couldn't find anyone to take us to work, we took the bus to and from, counting coins for the fare in the early mornings before it was time to grind. I'll never forget the day when my sister unknowingly dropped our coins somewhere on our way to the bus stop. The bus driver pulled over next to the cold metal bench where we'd been waiting for twenty minutes, opened the accordion door, and hailed us in. I was about to step on, when my sister hooked her arm around my elbow, pulled me back, and said, "We don't have enough money." We dropped to our knees and emptied our caddies and purses to rummage for coins that might have fallen through seams or between spray bottles. We turned our pockets inside out, and all we had was the pay-to-cash check our customer had left on the entryway console that morning and mints that I had taken from the house we cleaned the day before. The next bus wasn't to come until an hour later, and to miss this ride meant we wouldn't get to our next job on time and that we would have to wait in the cold. I heard the bus gear up to go again, and I looked at the bus driver with pleading eyes and put my hands together to motion *please*. He looked in the rearview mirror to see how many passengers he had, and he had only a few. He summoned us in with a tip of his chin.

What he did, his simple act of mercy, recalibrated a mechanism I had adopted when I was rejected, and nearly ejected, by a country. That is, the mechanism of always expecting the worst, a manifestation of chronic anxiety. When he kept the bus door open for us, he also held open a more-than-physical door. In my recent studies about PTSD and the mental health of immigrants, I learned that what I lost when I lost the ability to move was more than just physical faculty. When the immigration officer told me that even though I was adopted, I had aged out of naturalization benefits and was therefore unlawfully staying on American soil, my sense of America shifted from land of promise, as I had been told by people back home in the Philippines and by my new family in New York, to land of void. Most seventeen-year-old White and non-White Americans I knew began to drive handed-down cars. They began to experience a new kind of mobility. They researched universities, applied to those schools' programs, imagined their lives just far enough away from mom and dad so they could make their own choices. They imagined themselves independent. They imagined themselves participating in adulthood and citizenship. They imagined themselves enjoying liberties, carving out space for, and implanting their bodies in, projections of time and matter in their heads: What will they wear? What will their dorm rooms look like? Who will they befriend and date in college? Where will they intern? Where will they party? But at seventeen, my truth became the opposite. My dreams died. And with them, my body went, too. My mind became a perennial blank.

Because cleaning made my body sweat and my knuckles hurt and my eyes tear up, because the chemicals were so toxic I could taste them, because the repetition of small and big movements made my heart rate go up, cleaning revived me. Cleaning resuscitated what becoming undocumented killed.

When I was back to being fully functional, if any of us truly ever are fully functional, I cleaned with haste and vigor so I'd have time to read.

I brought library books to work and read them between chores or while I did one-handed jobs, such as dusting and Swiffering, or while I waited for my siblings to finish their tasks. A good portion of my energy went back into learning—reading when I couldn't attend school. By this time, my high school peers had been taking college courses for a full semester. I felt unstuck now, thanks to cleaning and to books, and I made a decision to find a way to move on. I found other jobs—doing people's laundry and working as an office assistant for a Filipino immigration lawyer. The lawyer gave me advice on my immigrant status and on how to go back to school. He coached me through the writing of a letter to the mayor of the Town of Hempstead, who, after a few months of my and the lawyer's petitioning, sent me an affidavit that stated that I was a resident of Nassau County, by way of adoption through one of its courts, and that I had at least one tax-paying adoptive parent and was therefore eligible for free or discounted services rendered by in-state universities. When the affidavit arrived at the law office, the attorney read it out loud many times, to every English-speaking and non-English-speaking client who came that day. He bought me a raspberry-glazed donut from Dunkin' Donuts that afternoon, and said, "Hija, you're going back to school."

That winter, I applied to the State University of New York's Fashion Institute of Technology, since I had focused on fashion design (as well as studio art and creative writing) at the art honors high school program. I already had a portfolio to submit and had an art teacher who wanted to write a recommendation. I received my acceptance letter in the spring and was to begin school the following autumn. In the months between acceptance and attendance, I tried to earn and save as much money as I could, working the three eight-hour days the lawyer could afford to hire me and working four seven-hour shifts at the laundromat.

———

I wish now that I could say that working at a laundromat with a drop-off service was as easy as dumping clothes into a washer, pouring in detergent, turning the dial, and pressing a button. I thought that was the job description when I walked in to interview on the spot with Miriam, the laundromat owner. She didn't enumerate the undertakings until after eighteen-year-old me had shaken her hand to accept the position. All she said was that if I could read instructions, I could do the job, and that the hourly pay was $6.50 plus tips—at least fifty cents more than what I was making cleaning houses. She also didn't check for an ID and said that she paid in cash. I perked up. When we sealed the deal, she took me to the drop-off kiosk at the back of the retail space, where an industrial weighing scale sat next to a table of forms. It had a graduation of up to two hundred and fifty pounds, large enough to weigh five children. I choked on my spit when I saw the scale and realized how much laundry I was to do each shift.

Miriam showed me the utility closet next, where she kept tubs of detergent powder, gallon jugs of Shout stain remover, spray bottles filled with a four-to-one ratio of water and Clorox, and a family-size mayonnaise jar that held different types of brushes: toothbrushes, dish brushes, brushes for cleaning grout, and a nozzle attachment taken from a vacuum cleaner. She explained which brush to use for which type or degree of stain, starting with the mildest: coffee stain, tomato-sauce stain, oil stain, and poop—wet, greenish-brown, soiled-in poop that contained all the ingredients that made up the other types of stains.

I came to my first day of work dreading the amount of laundry I had to do. When I clocked in, the person on shift before me, Maria, told me that the four mesh sacks to the left of the scale had to be laundered and folded by four o'clock. My shift started at one. I weighed the sacks and recorded the amount on the ledger (we charged by the pound)—a total of nearly two hundred pounds. I checked the last name of the customer, as Miriam had instructed me to always do first, and found the name written in all lowercase on the bags' tags: *l-o-n-g-o*. I will never forget the name. I made a rhyme of it in my head: *This day is gonna be long-o. This all seems so wrong-o.*

Longo's sacks were made of mesh, so I didn't have to open them to smell the mixture of food, bodily fluids, and poop that were entrenched in the fabrics. I asked Maria as she washed her hands clean of residue from garments and linens she had washed that day, how long each wash cycle was. She said each cycle was forty minutes long, then added, "Washing machine fits half a bag." If I had four sacks, it meant I needed eight washers. Out of the sixteen machines at the laundromat, Miriam reserved eight for self-service customers. That left me with four washers. I needed to do eight loads, and I had to soak and scrub the stained pieces before loading them into the washer, plus fold them after they had been dried—all in three hours.

"Start now, hija. You wastin' time," Maria said as she unhooked her bag from the back of the utility closet door.

I rolled a metal cart from the front of the laundromat to my station, emptied the contents of one of Longo's sacks into it, and sorted through. I gagged as I dug my hand into the clothes, the smell rising in clouds as I fluffed the pile to find the soiled pieces. Tears welled up as I tried not to breathe. *I can't do this,* I thought. But I remembered that I needed the money for college—New York City wasn't going to be cheap. I rummaged for gloves and disposable masks in the utility closet and found only a pair of dishwashing gloves that had been turned inside out from being snapped off someone's hand, the inside of them still sweaty. I rubbed them against my shorts to dry them before putting them on. Then I hid my mouth and nose in my shirt collar as I began to sort through the clothes again. I found several pieces of underwear, covered in brown and green and beige. I pinched the clean corners with index finger and thumb, transferred them to the sink where Miriam had told me to do the soaking and scrubbing, and squirted enough Shout onto the stains to hopefully make even my memories of this fade.

I put the first load into a washer and sorted another batch. I repeated the process of sorting, soaking, and loading, filling the four machines. While the machines ran, I scrubbed the pieces that had been soaking, first with a toothbrush, then the grout brush, and finally, for the more stubborn stains that wouldn't lighten in color, the vacuum cleaner attachment. I ran hot water over them, the gloves my only protection from the nastiness and the heat. I used my fingers to unclog the drain of underwear debris. When the machines buzzed to signal the first forty-minute round was up, I unloaded the wet clothes and transferred them into the dryers, checking the clock to see how much time I had left. I had about two hours. *This day is gonna be long-o.*

I did the sort-soak-load-scrub-dry process again for the remaining two sacks, and while I waited for the dryers to complete their cycles, I loaded the now-not-as-soiled pieces of underwear into a machine for a hot-water, heavy-duty cycle. I folded the dry items while I waited for the final wash, stacking clothes on every clean surface at the shop that wasn't being used by a self-service customer. I had to learn to fold in a two-vertical-crease by three-lateral-crease manner so the folded clothes would fit in the clear plastic bags they were sent home in. Nearing pickup time, I checked on the last load, transferred it into a dryer, and let it tumble. When the drying ended, I packed the last pieces, tied up the plastic bags, and stapled receipt copies onto each one. I sat down on the one stool we had by the drop-off kiosk, and before I could get comfortable, in walked a large man who puffed through his mouth to breathe, and who had sweat rings around his shirt collar and sleeve inseams.

"Pick up for Longo," he said, as he handed me cash. "Keep the change."

I deserve it, you filthy sir, I thought. "To the right of you, by the scale, six plastic bags. Don't forget your mesh sacks."

"You're new?"

I nodded.

"You're supposed to help me."

"I'm sorry?"

"I can't reach down. Help me get them off the floor." He couldn't reach down for the bags, couldn't even slightly bend at the knees. I understood then that this might have been a chronic problem—an inability that kept him from using the bathroom properly and from upkeeping his hygiene. This happened all the time for him. This batch of clothes was not an anomaly and he hadn't just been sick. He had a protocol he had established at pickup, which meant that he was a regular—his clothes and underwear were going to be a regular part of my job. I squatted down toward the bags and wrapped my arms around one, gathered it up with whatever was left of my energy that day, and walked the bags one by one to his car. After I'd loaded everything into his trunk, I walked back to the drop-off station, where two separate sets of laundry sat waiting. I checked the tags: *Pickup by end of shift.*

The last two sets I did that evening did not have stains, but the loading, unloading, transferring, and folding alone were enough to make me feel like I should quit my job. But I didn't. I kept showing up on my days off from the lawyer's office, because the job, while it was disgusting, exhausting, and demeaning, did not require an ID or a valid work visa. I had to keep it to save money for school, so I could one day get a job that wouldn't make me gag.

———

When I moved on to college, my sister moved on to a nanny job. She worked for a half-Filipino cousin who worked in finance—for whom she took care of one, then two, then three newborns. The children attached to her like I did to my childhood yaya—my nanny—and they cried every evening when she put on her shoes to get ready to go home, the middle one especially. She had three children of her own by this point, so in all, she had six to pray and wrap Christmas presents for, six to keep her from falling completely asleep at night. My sister told me once, "When you become a mom, you only half sleep. You think of your kids through the night."

When my sister entered this profession, she also entered an ever-growing group of women in our family who spent their days caring for other people's kids, sick, and elderly. All these women—titas, ates, manangs, lolas, nanays—each had at least one academic degree and two children of their own. Most of them worked for Manhattan families. While I boarded in a Harlem apartment shared with two Viennese girls, the yayas in my family took the Long Island Rail Road every morning before six, arrived in the city by seven, walked or took the subway to their employers' homes in SoHo, Chelsea, the West Village, the Upper East or West Side, TriBeCa, or the Financial District. They started work before the children's parents left for their jobs, usually around eight in the morning, and stayed until either the mom or the dad came home that night. Sometimes they stayed extra hours, should the parents need a date night or have a work dinner—an eleven- to fifteen-hour workday. This meant the yayas saw their own children infrequently or briefly. My nephews, nieces, and cousins learned how to take care of themselves because Mama wasn't home. My nephew, Enrico, learned to cook dinner and bake dessert, sometimes selling his cakes for supplementary income. My niece, Adrianna, acted as the family driver, babysitter, and grocery shopper.

I came to work with my ates Magda and Ligaya once, both nannies for preschoolers. We met at Chelsea Market, where the kids could run down the halls in a somewhat confined space, and where we could each pay for a snack item to share. I bought dumplings, Magda got french fries, and Ligaya a bag of sweet brioche. We ate the snacks family-style, the kids sitting in their strollers that were parked next to the table. I watched Magda and Ligaya hand-feed the children, wipe off dumpling juice dribbling down their chins, and blow hot steam from the fries. One of the kids, who sat on the skateboard attachment to one of the strollers, got up to hug Ligaya around the neck. He kissed her cheek and said, "Love you, yaya."

"'Wag malikot. Sit down please, Marcel," Ligaya said, sternly but sweetly, in a mix of Tagalog and English, so that the words came out singsongy but striking—how most Filipina moms I know speak. This is how I find myself speaking to my daughter now. "Finish your food, okay? Sige na."

Marcel immediately sat back down, stuck two fingers in his piece of brioche, and played with it like a finger puppet before plunging it into his wide-open mouth. "Yum, yum, Mama Ligaya gives me good food."

"Yaya, not mama," Ligaya corrected. She turned to me and Magda. "Naku, he will get me in trouble with his mother. I've told him not to call me that."

"Ay, ako rin. I told this one the same thing," Magda said of her charge.

I've heard my sister and many other Filipina nannies say this same thing—that their charges call them *mom*, *mommy*, or *mama*. I've seen these children cling to their yayas' legs like a sloth hanging from a limb, stalling the departure of their beloved caretaker at the end of the workday. The mothers, whom I saw through the doorway as I waited in the hall for my aunt and cousin, crossed and uncrossed their arms, unsure whether to assert authority, to be soft, or to act apathetically. Despite the routine awkwardness, the parents continued to employ the yayas— after all, a woman who could cook, hush a baby, help with homework, teach manners, implement and enforce otherwise throwaway house and playground rules, and listen to the parents' venting about professional and personal woes was a prime commodity in the city. For ten dollars or less per hour, a New York family could have its own baby whisperer, personal chef, therapist, tutor, chauffeur, and substitute grandmother or godmother—sans any judgment from others. The pay was—and remains—low because a majority of the yayas are undocumented.

But my being undocumented did not matter when I applied for a nanny job during my last year in college. By this point, I had worked as a tutor, hostess, server, fashion-showroom help, personal assistant, and archival researcher. In my last two college years, though, I was playing catch-up after transferring from fashion school to journalism school. I needed to graduate on time because costs kept increasing, and because I had met a boy I wanted to follow to Athens, Georgia, the summer after graduation. To finish by May 2009, I had to take on twenty-one credits per semester—which is about two classes more than the recommended load. All my previous jobs required that I worked at least six hours a day, so when a friend told me that a family she worked for on Wall Street needed a nanny for only three hours each weekday morning and three hours on Saturday nights, I asked that she call in my recommendation. The mother, an Australian housewife who wanted a couple of hours each morning to walk to the park, shop, or meet a friend, and whose husband worked for an investment bank, interviewed me for fifteen minutes. She asked how I knew the person who recommended me, and, of course, if I had any experience caring for children.

"Yes, I—"

She cut me off. "Great! Now you're in school, yes? Carrie told me you studied writing and art."

"Art history, actually."

"Fantastic! I did, too! My husband's the boring one. Finance. *Uck.*" She talked with an energetic voice, pitchy and onomatopoeic, but with her hands folded on her lap. That's how I would always remember her: body constrained but dying to talk. "Emily's the little one, and she'll be with you in the mornings—a stroll and a nap. So bring a magazine . . . or a textbook!"

I grinned. I was going to get paid to sit and read.

"Fifteen okay?"

"I'm sorry?"

"Fifteen an hour. Is that low?" She frowned.

Fifteen dollars was higher than any hourly rate I had been paid before, except for the server job. But I didn't get to sit and read at the restaurant. Now I was to listen to a baby breathe in her crib, while I splayed on the couch and read, for five dollars more per hour than my yaya counterparts were making. I wondered if it was my American accent, or my knowledge of the collections at the Met, or the Michael Kors tunic I had on that Ligaya salvaged from her employer's Goodwill pile, that qualified me for a higher pay. I didn't ask, but I wanted to know who set the rate, and why, and for whom.

Was fifteen dollars the rate given to young girls who were more au pairs than nannies, and what was the difference between the two? What did the five-dollar difference sound and look like: Anglicized? Americanized? More international than immigrant? Young? Nannying was a kind of starter job for me, and a last straw for my sister, aunties, and cousins. Was that the difference—that this was a springboard, hopefully, to my future work, but it was an end-all-be-all for the yayas? They had fallen from grace, as some would have put it. And they were, to look at it from a flawed human resources perspective, too old, too burdened—*mothers*—to recover now, more liability than asset. But if I could just figure out how to legalize my stay in the US, I was on the rise. I never told Emily's mother that I was an undocumented adoptee who entered the US as an unaccompanied minor. I was afraid that the knowledge would change her perception of me—that it would bring down my paycheck, that she would stop talking to me like I was a friend she could take to an art gallery. And for me, did five dollars equate to the price of pride? *I'm a nanny for a family on Wall Street.* Did the extra five dollars mean more than just coffee or rent money—did it buy me back the sense of worth I lost when I found out that I had lost legal status?

Pushing Emily in one of those coffee-cup-holding, shock-absorbing, phone-charging, one-click-folding, four-hundred-dollar baby strollers down Pearl Street one morning, I brushed past a gaggle of yayas on a walk with their charges. I smiled at one of them as we crossed paths, and she smiled back and said to her friends, "Kolehiyala." College girl. Then she pointed at me not with her finger but with puckered lips, the way we learn to point or give direction in the Philippines. Her kumares turned to me in unison, grinned, and said, "Mag-aral kang mabuti." An instruction to study well. But also an instruction to make the most of my time here in America, to get a job better than this, to secure my lot and that of my family. I wanted to tell them, *I will, I promise. But I'm undocumented like you. I will study as hard as I can, but who knows what I'll actually be able to do.* But I didn't say it. I just waved and said, "Opo," our polite way of saying yes. I didn't say what I wanted to say because I didn't want to disappoint them. Young ones like me were the reason why they came here, why they wiped noses and butts, why they endured being away from our culture and family and home. They looked forward to my accomplishments, to seeing me own a car, a home, maybe a business. And every morning that I ran into them, the Wall Street yayas waved at me, gave the same instruction, and blessed me. Pag-palain ka ng Diyos. May God prosper you. And every morning I waved back, receiving both command and blessing.

I kept my out-of-status a secret from Emily's family and from the Wall Street yayas for an entire school year—September 2008 through June 2009. I wanted to hold on to the confidence Emily's mother had in me, the ease with which she could speak to me about lofty matters like art and music and politics, and about everyday matters like laundry and what to wear and what to cook. I wanted her to keep passing on copies of *Time* and the *New Yorker*. I wanted her to keep asking me if I'd seen the new exhibit at the MoMA, or if she should wear her new Marchesa dress to the gala, or if I thought she was "just a pathetic homemaker." I also wanted the yayas to brim with excitement every time they saw me. I wanted them to keep teasing me and calling out to me from across the street, "Hello, Miss New York Times!" I wanted them to hold on to the idea that a young Filipina could maybe, *maybe*, one day write about the Filipino immigrant experience—that maybe, *maybe*, one day, someone would write about them and acknowledge their sacrifices.

I graduated on my twenty-third birthday, on May 28, 2009, at the peak of the Great Recession. By then, some of the yayas in my family had lost their jobs because their employers had lost theirs. It felt right for me to move down South and follow my boyfriend; New York was so badly hit by the recession that nobody—documented or undocumented—could get a job. Emily's family had decided to move to Canada, where her father could start anew by managing portfolios for the newly moneyed. On my last day of working for their family, I saw only half of the Wall Street yayas. I assumed that their employers had been badly hit by the recession, too.

I took a train to Philadelphia, then hitched a ride to Athens, Georgia, just two weeks after graduation. I took with me the same rip-off Tommy Hilfiger duffel bag that I had come to America with, plus a granny cart I purchased from a stall in Chinatown, and my savings of $3,700—enough to rent a bedroom in Athens for ten months plus a couple hundred for emergencies. Emily's mother cried to me on the phone before I left for the South and they left for Toronto, telling me that I was the best caregiver they ever had. I told her I would keep in touch. And she told me she wished for me to write a book and to see it at a bookstore one day. I thanked her for having been kind to me and said that I was sorry for all the changes coming her way. But still, I didn't say that I was without papers, that I might never publish a book because I didn't have a social security number or valid ID. It was best to keep everybody's hopes up—because I knew what it was like to be hopeless. I knew that hopelessness could halt you, make your body stop.

———

I arrived in Athens only to be told that nobody was going to hire me because this was the South, and in the South, people loved their conservative ways and their conservative rules. A bar manager told me this as he unstacked chairs for that night's live music event. I told him I had worked as a hostess at a restaurant, a cocktail waitress at a speakeasy, and a barista at a café. I told him I was a good cook, that I was from a family of cooks. He still said no, he couldn't give me a job.

"This is the South."

I felt my body start to freeze again, just like when my immigration papers were rejected—my toes gluing together, my neck stiffening. "I'm a hard worker. I will work harder than any of these college kids in town. I'll do anything. I'll care for your customers like it's nobody's business."

"Sorry, babe."

I went to the next bar and the next boutique. "No. Sorry," they told me.

My roommate at the time was a Pennsylvania girl who wanted to leave Amish country. She'd been sewing all her life and had made a corset that I would later wear to a Halloween party. She fitted me in the corset, marking the hem with tailor's chalk, inserting boning into splits in the seams. Before moving to Athens, she had worked at many bars. She was done working night shifts and around drunks, she told me as she tugged at the corset to make it tighter. With only an associate's degree and no work experience outside of bartending, she, too, had a hard time finding a job.

Desperate, I made a proposal. "Gigi, what if we started a business together? You're really good at sewing. Look at this intricate work. What if we started a custom-order business?"

"I am *not* going to make wedding dresses. I've seen enough of those bridezilla shows."

"No, exactly, we do the opposite. We make things for the grooms. Nobody ever makes stuff for the guys." I was excited at this prospect—to delve into fashion again, to make sketches like I used to in the art honors high school program. I felt giddy thinking about working with my hands—but without mops, brushes, or rags.

"I'm done caring for men's egos. I did that at bars. So exhausting."

"Not egos. Just ties. They pick a color, fabric, and style. That's it. Minimal interaction and all online."

I set up an Etsy account the following morning and took photos of neckwear she had previously made. I posted the photos and labeled them as made-to-order pieces that were handmade by two girls living in Georgia and perfect for grooms and groomsmen. Within hours, we had multiple clicks and an inquiry. The first message contained two questions: *Can you make twelve bow ties out of my Scottish clan tartan? Can you make them within two weeks?*

"Gigi! We have a customer!"

"What customer?"

"I made an online listing and this guy wants his wedding bow ties custom-made!"

She walked from her room to mine, crouched over my laptop, and read the message twice, thrice, and didn't speak as she walked back to her room.

"You're mad?"

She popped her head back in. "Tell him we're not responsible for any damages to his clan tartan."

Over the next ten months, we made bow ties, neckties, and ascots for grooms from all around the world—from Germany and Scotland to Alabama and the Pacific Northwest. I took $200 from my savings of $3,700, and with it purchased materials for lining and interlining. We received shipments of either heirloom or new fabric, but always material that carried sentiment or history, and turned the cloths into bespoke accessories that either brides gifted to their would-be spouses or grooms to their closest male friends and relatives, and to themselves. At the time, nobody else in the bridal market specialized in such products.

Online magazines featured us in their pages and bridal networking sites rated us as *New and Noteworthy*.

Gigi spent two full days making patterns for each order, and another full day cutting them. Depending on the number of ties and the complexity of the pattern—pin tucked, knife pleated, color blocked, honeycombed—Gigi spent three to ten days sewing. I did the finishing touches such as embroidering initials or names, stitching in buttonholes and clasps, and, believe it or not, beadwork—hundreds of beads. When I wasn't embroidering or embellishing, I canvassed materials, processed orders, designed and placed online ads, sent invoices, received payments, shipped packages, and replied to emails. When we offered the world of men's bridal fashion an opportunity to let guys contribute their visions and tastes to wedding planning, the men did not hold back. It was as though grooms had been wanting to flaunt their style down the aisle, too, and finally, two girls in their bedrooms in Georgia could make their dreams come true. Beyond simply building an accessory brand, we made a business out of caring for, and carrying out, men's bridal aspirations. We made them look dapper on their wedding day, gave them and their guests something to talk about, and made tangible a part of their personalities that likely had yet to surface. A preacher's son wore a hand-painted camo-and-forest-green skinny tie. A poet said *I do* with a line by Wordsworth embroidered close to his heart. A marine donned a coral-and-cream bow tie made out of Liberty of London's quintessential floral calico. A farmer sported a baby-blue chevron print.

To streamline the collaborative design process, I made an online questionnaire for our clients to fill out. It was my mistake to leave the responses open-ended, as opposed to short answer or multiple choice, because when asked, *What do you envision for your bridal neckwear?*, the grooms wrote paragraph upon paragraph, not only about aesthetic or fabric, but also about their lives. They shared stories about childhood, religion, work, their engagement, the battles they'd won at court, in combat, on wheelchairs, or in hospital beds. The preacher's son who wanted camo and forest green wrote that he wanted a tie to remind him of both his time in the military and his time as a missionary in the jungles of Brazil. A Manhattan socialite with a Park Avenue address asked that we make him and his bridal party neckties that resembled the sculptural details from works he grew up admiring with his late father—that we make him a tie with a three-dimensional design, which we translated as finger pleats that created an undulating illusion when turned from side to side. We also received stories about miscarriages, previous marriages, the unfortunate effects of the Great Recession on family businesses. From these ramblings and confessions, I sketched one-of-a-kind mock-ups. Back and forth the emails went—tweaks on, and evolutions from, the initial drafts.

By our tenth month, Gigi and I had grown short-tempered and cantankerous with one another, depleted of physical and mental strength by a business that required both expected meticulous craftsmanship and unexpected emotional labor. I often wondered if our clients poured out their concerns to us because their brides were too busy with other aspects of their nuptials.

My eyesight worsened tenfold, Gigi developed carpal tunnel syndrome, and the business did not make enough to afford us health insurance. On top of the bitterness we felt toward our jobs and then projected onto one another, I got engaged. I would have to move out and leave the room I was renting, and she and the landlord would need to find a new renter. She was happy for me, she said, but she fretted over what to do next. After all, we had been using my room as an office, storage unit, and photography studio. And we had been able to keep our rates moderate because we didn't pay rent on a facility. We had a meeting in the hallway between our two bedrooms to talk about how we could keep the business alive, or if we should at all. And in the end, after the crying and yelling and finger-pointing, we commiserated with one another. We decided that the business was burdensome in every way, and that we would rather salvage our friendship than salvage the business.

The boy I followed to the South gave me a ring made out of his mother's and aunt's jewelry, and while I wanted to elope, he suggested we have a real wedding. I told him, "I'm so over weddings," another displacement of negative emotions from my work into a personal relationship. He said that he knew me well enough, that he knew I would enjoy designing a day for myself and for us, and that I would regret not having a celebration with family and friends.

We compromised and planned for an eight-week engagement and a fifty-person ceremony in New York, at Central Park. And he was right. I absolutely loved our wedding—the wildflowers in mason jars, the sparrows in the birdbath, the cupcakes our friends baked, the couch we sat on in the middle of the sunlit greenery, and the dancing. But my most favorite part of all, despite the number of times I had said that I'd learned to hate sewing and fashion because of the business, was my wedding dress. Gigi tailored an empire-waist sheath out of Cuban lace given to me by a dear friend from Jamaica. Like the fabrics we made into ties, the lace had a story, and into it, I wove mine. I drafted a sketch of my dream dress, scanned it, and emailed it to Gigi, and the masterwork became our last project together—a rather joyful end to a partnership that had grown sour. She moved back to Pennsylvania, and I moved in with my groom. We sold the business to a friend dying to jump out of the garment-industry circus, and to her we mailed leftover lining and interlining, fabric, small tools, and a new embroidery machine preprogrammed to stitch designs made on the computer. The machine was supposed to replace my handicraft, and it was another previous point of contention between Gigi and me: Was it fair to market the ties as handmade if the last step of our process involved digitization and machinery? Was it ethical if we adopted a small mechanization to lighten our load and be gentler on our eyes and fingers and time? The friend who purchased the business from us cared not a single bit about this—a nonissue compared to dealings within the commercial market, she said. A few months after settling into our new lives, Gigi and I talked briefly through texts, consoled each other, and apologized. We agreed then that the problem was not the process, nor the clients, nor the machines. The problem was that we both cared too much.

———

I got pregnant the following April, just six months after the wedding. I lay on the floor when the stick showed two lines, instead of the single line I was hoping for. My new husband and I had spent our first half year as a married couple looking for jobs, as he was to finish graduate school at the end of the spring semester. Still unable to secure a full-time position because of my undocumented status, I worked part-time for the stationery store below our apartment. The storeowner let us live in the apartment, which was the store's attic, in exchange for copywriting and calligraphy. I worked with my hands again, but this time on a much less taxing task: penning names and addresses on envelopes.

It took two weeks to accept the pregnancy as our new reality, and it was friends who said "I'm so sorry," as opposed to "You should be happy," that helped us get to that point. Those who understood how bleak the future seemed for us were the people that comprehended how difficult it would be for me, especially, to earn a paycheck while still completing the process of applying for permanent resident status *and* taking care of a baby. I hadn't worked in a field related to my bachelor's degree, so while my undocumented life was about to end, thanks to my marriage, I didn't have a résumé. I didn't have the internships. I was cleaning houses, washing and folding laundry, and nannying instead. I hadn't learned trade language and practices from a postcollege starter position. I was operating what resembled a two-person sweatshop out of my bedroom. And now I was affording my graduate-student husband and myself room and board by utilizing the perfect penmanship

I had brought with me from my Philippine Catholic-school training. Nothing I had done looked good on paper; I had no paper trail of accomplishments. Being undocumented meant that while I had poured my sweat and soul into jobs, and more importantly, into people, none of my work—my *care*—mattered. In America, I learned to believe, humans were only as valuable as the numbers and positions typed up on their résumés and LinkedIn profiles. Humans equated only to returns on investment, to demographics that campaign managers needed to assess and reach. I came to America as a teenage adoptee, hopeful after having escaped a life with a negligent and mentally ill mother, an absent father, an abusive stepfather, and their friends and foes who had made life dangerous for me. I came here thinking that I would smooth-sail into high school and college, then into a job, and maybe along the way afford myself whatever was necessary to recuperate from the trauma back home. Instead, I was seventeen and frozen under a spell of acedia. I was eighteen and wondering if I would only ever be a domestic. I was twenty-three and questioning my every effort at obtaining an education: *What was even the point?* Then I was twenty-five, about to have a baby, about to be stuck at home to change diapers and nurse all day, and maybe never be able to get a "real" job because, as a friend who was ten years ahead of me in age and in life had said, employers avoided hiring mothers.

But I was a very good pregnant woman. I had no difficulty caring for my body those thirty-seven weeks of gestation. I ate the same Greek-yogurt-and-egg-white breakfast every morning; drank the same protein-and-kale smoothie for lunch; and consumed a high-fiber, high-nutrient, lean-protein dinner every night. I took thirty-minute walks first thing upon waking up and walked again before going to bed. The added weight and midsection pressure exacerbated the bad back I had developed from scrubbing tiles, so I took on a prenatal yoga routine I found on YouTube. I told myself that if I could follow the rules of pregnancy, I could show the world that I could apply myself to other things; that if I could take steps toward something, I could take steps toward the political freedom for which I'd been waiting and striving for nearly ten years.

I borrowed books about pregnancy, childbirth, infant health, newborn sleep habits, and gentle discipline, because while I was secluded from the White, suburban mom scene, I always had books to turn to for advice and company. Books did not discriminate, at least not explicitly. Books did not ask for my background. While some books I picked up from the library did seem to have been written for a certain kind of mother—upper-middle-class, White, stay-at-home women with little to no concern about their health, finances, or immigrant status— I could speed-read through the passages that didn't resonate with me. Reading during pregnancy rekindled my love of books. Apart from the pregnancy and parenting titles I checked out from the library, I read books that appealed to me: prose about young women of color or young women who had encountered some form of trauma—which, in 2011, was not all that ubiquitous. The search for these types of books added to the thrill.

I took this reading habit into early motherhood. Our baby girl was born at thirty-seven weeks and weighed five pounds, just a little too small to not have to see the doctor every two days but a little too big to be in an incubator in the NICU. We were homebound from the very beginning for frequent feedings and to avoid threats to her immune system. I grieved the fact that she was so small, because I felt like I had done everything the books told me to do and yet, there she was, in need of extra care. It felt like a mirroring of my life as a student—I had taken every step, I had read every book, I had worked toward every A and A+, and yet.

Away from my family in New York and without a network of close friends, I again turned to books for advice and company. When I sat down to feed my baby girl, who refused the bottle and only wanted to nurse, I read. I cried, too. I thought my baby was the most beautiful baby I'd ever seen: dark hair and eyes and a little nose like mine, a dimpled chin and a wide forehead like her father's. But no matter how much I adored her and how much a part of me felt awakened when I held her, I also felt benumbed. Not that parts of me died when she was born, but that I had suddenly become aware of my dead parts. When I held her, I only let the tears trickle, afraid that even as young as she was, she could perceive my sadness and possibly take it upon herself. When she slept or when her father nestled her in the crook of his arm or on his chest, and I could step far enough away that they couldn't hear me, I sobbed in the bathroom or in the closet, heaving like I used to when I cleaned toilets and scrubbed soiled underwear. Sometimes I tried to muffle my cries by squatting between clothes on hangers, wiping my snot on the sleeves of my husband's shirts and stuffing my mouth with the cuffs to stifle the sound.

When the baby let him put her down in the crib or bouncy seat, my husband pulled me out of the closet or bathroom and to our bed, where he'd tuck me in, tell me to rest, and pray while he held my hand. I'd fall asleep just to wake up to cry again. At our two-week postnatal checkup, I told the nurse practitioner that I often felt anxious or sad and asked if I needed medication. She said that because I could still talk through my feelings and was aware of my emotional state, that perhaps it was just the baby blues—that the sadness would go away at six weeks postbirth. But the blues didn't leave. The blues just turned black.

Newborn care felt heavy, as I had expected it to be, because I had seen my sister care for three infants of her own and three of another mother's. But the heaviness I felt came with the weight of always expecting the worst: the nonending work of caring for others, the pattern of giving your all and not receiving anything in return. I described my state as more of a grieving than a depression when I talked to my husband, and for this he lovingly prescribed that I write again. I had just read an essay about how new mothers who are trauma survivors are more likely than other women to develop postpartum depression and a new onset of complex PTSD symptoms. While the nurse practitioner believed that all I was experiencing was hormonal change, my husband, who knew about my distant past in the Philippines and my recent past as an immigrant, suggested that I pay attention to how pain and grief were manifesting: aches in my lower back and right leg, hair loss, chest tightness, constant sobbing, irritability, an atypical inability to laugh or make someone laugh—it was my sense of humor he was first drawn to when we met in 2006.

"I think you should write it all out," he said.

"I don't write anymore. I'm not a writer. I'll never be one now."

"Not true. Start small." He gave me a pack of three-by-five-inch index cards from CVS and told me that because I thrived on routine, I should write a word or phrase or paragraph every time I sat down to nurse the baby. "You have to nurse her every two hours anyway." Our baby nursed slowly, about forty minutes to get her fill. That made for at least eight times per day in the rocking chair of forty minutes each—more time to write than I have now as a "professional." The index cards fit perfectly on the armrests of the rocking chair, and the chair did not rock because it was situated on carpet. I could sit and be still with my thoughts and memories. There, I turned to my past—stories and names and mental images that flooded in as though a gate had been broken open. Everything I had run away from, that had thrust me onto a plane to San Francisco, then to New York, stormed into the heather-gray and honeycomb-yellow nursery. My baby's room felt wet with Manila rainwater—my own childhood intruding into my child's. My body had given birth to a human, but my body also wanted to expel something more. It wanted to flush out the accumulation of hurt and sorrow and fear, three things all immigrants pack with them from home. No longer trapped in acedia, no longer compartmental-ized so I could work and survive, my memories let out onto paper and bled onto the page as words, phrases, sentences, paragraphs. In those forty-minute breastfeeding sessions, I could nurture my girl and kindle my memories. By the time my sweet baby was a year and a half old, I had three shoeboxes full of index cards—what would become puzzle pieces formed into a synopsis, then an annotated table of contents, and finally, a manuscript submitted to a master of fine arts in creative writing program, and to an agent and editor. I named the book after my childhood home, but also the storm—the monsoons—I had weathered.

I wrote. I wrote and cared for myself for the very first time. I went to therapy soon after my baby's second birthday, and with my therapist, I wrote more and read my work out loud. I authored a memoir, and while thousands of readers think of it as a tale of triumph over my past, I see it now as having triumphed over my future. Because I confronted my trauma, in all its repetitions and demonstrations, big and small, I learned myself. I heard a pastor say once, "To be known is to be loved; to be loved is to be known." I had not known myself fully until I wrote my story, which meant I had shortchanged myself of love. I had cared for people's homes, babies, food, clothes, weddings, and stories. But I had not tended to myself. When reporters and readers ask why I write memoir or nonfiction, or why I went through the painstaking work of writing a book about my most traumatic experiences, I tell them that I did it because it was a way to love myself. I didn't do it because I wanted to be spiteful toward my parents, or because I wanted to make money by sensationalizing my history and politics. I wanted to do it and I needed to do it because I needed looking after. I wrote to be well.

———

A friend and fellow author I met at a writing residency, Zeyn Joukhadar, invited me to speak on a panel and debut our books together at the Strand Book Store, a New York literary establishment. Reading with us that night was Hala Alyan, a novelist whose short and long works I'd admired. Nervous about releasing my memoir, but also nervous about speaking to what I assumed was a highbrow crowd, and among writers who'd accomplished far more than I had academically or professionally, I packed a bag of totems to keep calm. The bag itself was a *Literary Hub* tote given to me by a publicist at my publishing imprint, and it pictured Joan Didion's face on the front—my nonfiction heroine. Inside the bag was my Philippine passport, a reminder of how long and far I'd traveled to get to the point where I would read a passage from my book to a crowd. The bag also contained a Polaroid of my six-year-old, the baby I nursed while I wrote, and a passport photo of my husband, whose idea it was to start small with index cards. Lastly, I packed a laminated bookmark made of recycled paper with a watercolor illustration of a woman in an empire-waist dress—a dress similar to what I wore on my wedding day. I purchased that bookmark on December 17, 2004, as I noted on the back of the bookmark, the evening following a bad day at work. I had been tasked with cleaning the basement of a woman's home that morning, but because I had gotten distracted by a book I had taken to work that day, I neglected to dust under the television console—the first and only time I messed up on the job. The woman decided that my cleaning fee had to be cut, and so I did not have enough money to purchase a book that night. I had planned on buying a used copy of one of Jessica Hagedorn's books, but only had enough cash for a postcard or a bookmark. I chose the bookmark since it was reusable and, with an urge coming from a still and small voice in or around me that night, wrote on it, *December 17, 2004. One Step Closer.* I did not know what step I was taking, nor to where or what I was heading closer. I just knew that the little hope I still had was enough to push me forth.

On May 2, 2018, the day after the official release of my debut, I read to an audience and answered questions. I discussed mental health, immigration, trauma, and the politics of the body with two of the most intelligent people I had ever met. I signed books. I hugged people who said that they finished my memoir in a day, said that it inspired them, that it held them or wrangled them, or made them feel seen and less alone. I gave advice to a girl who asked how she could, as an undocumented, write her own story one day. I said, "Remember you got grit. Press on."

When the bookstore cleared of people, I shook the hand of the manager in charge of the event. I showed him the bookmark and told him the long, meandering story about it.

He said, "Wow. Can I see it closer?"

I handed him the bookmark, which he flipped over back and forth, amused at how intact it was. He kept opening his mouth, trying to say something other than *wow*, but all he could muster was, "Wow. I can't believe it. Just wow. I am so happy for you."

I am happy for me, too.

Café Culture

Springtime

"How could you stay?" my friend Nina whispers as she cuts a fingerling potato with a butter knife. Her blonde curls bounce as she chews.

How could I not? I want to say back. Staying, leaving—it is a decision I need to make about my place of work. And I mean that word: *place*. Most college students I know, including Nina, refer to their employment as a job or a gig or, more seriously, an internship. They work *for* a company; I work *at* a place. And this place is the setting for many stories. This is one of them.

"Please stay out of trouble," she says with one brow raised. "I'd miss you if you got deported."

I grin and take a sip of my almond milk mocha, a beverage I learned to drink only fifteen months back, when I started working at this brick-walled, sunlit café. Before working here, I had never liked coffee, much less espresso, not even for the warm smell. "I need to gulp this down. Shift's about to start."

"Look at you. A coffee gulper. Where did my tea-only friend go?"

I guzzle my drink and lick my lips as I collect the mug and table-ware I used for my free meal. I hold up the mug as if to give a toast, and, after rolling her eyes, Nina raises hers, too. As I walk away, I can feel her look around and judge the place, the modern decor, the chalkboard menu, the waitstaff, and me, but I don't turn back to explain myself. I take my black canvas apron from the hook behind the bar, wrap the straps twice around my waist, and knot it hard and tight, pulling at the loops and ends—each tug punctuating my thoughts: *She'll never get it. I need this job. I love it here.*

The Summer Before

Sean, the general manager, interviewed me. We sat across from each other on metal chairs that I had seen in a hipster magazine feature called "Industrial Chic." I had never worked at a café and wasn't a coffee drinker, though I enjoyed the coffee shop scene—I was a Manhattanite studying art and literature, a mainstay at these somewhat communal living rooms and another broke kid who would forgo meals to afford a five-dollar drink: rent for a seat in a space filled with a conjured intellectual yet laissez-faire air. I fit the picture, with my cat-eye glasses, tote bag of books, oversize vintage Lacoste cardigan, skinny jeans, and Earl Grey latte. I emphasized this when Sean asked why I wanted to work at Café Culture. "I fit right in."

"Yeah, but what else? And I don't care if you don't drink coffee. You'll learn." He gingerly folded my application in half, and another half, with his huge fingers. Sean looked like he loved the gym: his pecs pressed through the thin white cotton of the stretchy shirt under his tight blazer. But he also hadn't stopped smiling—at me, at the customers, at the busboy he called over to wipe the table. "What can you add to this place? Me, I'm a life coach, too."

He swished an arm in a semicircle, gesturing to his home away from home, which was six blocks north on Frederick Douglass and one block west toward Columbia University. I looked at all his pretty café things and pretty café people. Before I could answer, he spoke again. Still smiling, he named each one of his full-time employees: Neja, a singer from Denmark with a voice to charm; Lukas, a conservatory-trained

Viennese actor who was balancing three glasses in one hand; Devonte, who had just wiped down our table and who, in Sean's words, was the only true Harlemite among us because he and his mama were both born on this side of Central and Morningside Parks; a dreadlocked ex-convict who went by O and whose real name nobody knew; E. J., also formerly in prison and who now ran the exposed subway-tiled kitchen, and who chewed on a toothpick while he impatiently delivered a plate that neither Neja nor Lukas were, despite their front-of-the-house confidence, quick enough to take from the kitchen; and Odilia, a statuesque German African American who presided over the quick tiff between the kitchen and the floor.

"See what I mean? Odilia resolves issues at the café and on the phone. Neja and Lukas can both work a busy floor, and I mean *work it*. My boys in the back cook, but they also keep us safe, like security guards. You, what are you good at?"

I knew my strength, used it like a crutch. "I'm really nice and people trust me."

He tapped his ear twice and pointed up. "Say that again. Louder."

"I'm nice and—"

"And?"

"And on your busy hours, like brunch, I'd make a great hostess." I had grown up believing that this was my job. My father, always gone but affectionate when around, repeatedly told me that I was the darling of our house, that I kept him and Mama happy even as our family business and their marriage went awry.

"How's that different than what Odilia does?" Sean said, biting into a red-velvet waffle too overdone to serve to a customer.

I told him that Odilia supervised kitchen and floor staff, but I, my father's words still ringing in my ears, would keep the customers happy. I had stood in line to eat there on a recent Sunday morning, and had waited almost an hour for a coveted table. Speaking from experience, I told Sean that the worst part of dining there was the wait and the lack of someone who could buffer it. The café was packed, but he was sitting with me. He could have taken my application and called me at the number I listed on it, but instead he was interviewing me on the spot. He should have been helping Neja and Lukas run or take orders. "I complimented you on your watch. You're wearing a Fossil, but I made you feel like it was a Cartier."

He nodded slowly, like he was jamming to an old song. "I like you. Come back on Sunday at nine."

I shook his hand and we smiled at each other. Smiling, beaming, expressing friendliness—something we were both good at. He added, "Keep the fashion thing going on. I'm hiring you to be nice and look nice, we clear?"

I said yes, but that I had another question. "I, uh, I don't have papers."

He tapped his ear twice again.

"I don't have papers," I said a little louder. The people at the table next to us looked over, then looked away.

"Of course you don't," Sean laughed. "Many of these fuckers don't either. Part of the charm of this place, ain't it?" As if on cue, and as if they'd been part of the conversation all along, Neja, Lukas, and Odilia turned their heads to us. Now we were all smiling.

Sean picked up his plate, pushed his seat back to get up, and said, "Learn to speak up, though, got it?"

I came back that Sunday in a zebra-print H&M dress for my first on-the-job training. Sean showed me where my apron, the water pitcher and glasses, and the menus and clipboard lived. He asked for my three favorite numbers, which he punched into the POS system as my employee PIN for clocking in. "Clock in, eat your server meal, check yourself in the bathroom mirror—no spinach or anything in your teeth." He grabbed a clipboard from under the bar and showed me how to make a waiting list. "Make sure both servers on shift get equal tables. Remember your job description?"

"Be nice and look nice."

He walked me to the front door, where I was to stand for weeknight dinner service and weekend brunch hours. He said to seat the customers first—*guests*—then hand them the menus. Before they could read through it from front to back, I had to fill their water glasses and tell them their server's name. "Brunch starts in fifteen. Line's gonna get long. Work your magic."

The line had wrapped around the side of the building by the time Sean flipped the "Open/Closed" sign. I pushed open the door and held it for the first customers, a couple clutching a thick wad of reading material: the Style section of the Sunday *Times* and a glossy copy of *Dwell Magazine* that featured a glass-walled mountain cabin on the cover. Clothing, spaces—they were easy to connect with.

"Sunday Styles entertaining and informative so far?" I asked the woman as I topped off her glass with water.

"It's one or the other nowadays, isn't it?" she said, loudly but dryly, making her eyes big to match the obvious answer she knew I was looking for but speaking with lazy lips to retain her coolness.

I gave her my currency: my smile. "Your server today is Neja. Enjoy your reading and your meal."

The rest of the day would be just like this quick exchange. I found a point of connection and made Harlem familiar with a compliment or question. My work, while it seemed superficial, possibly even fake, was necessary for the café and its patrons and the context we were in: Café Culture, one of the first cafés in South Harlem. In fact, one of the first of a boom of restaurants to flood that stretch above 110th Street. Culture—what a perfect name for a place with large communal wooden tables and an espresso machine; run by a life and gym coach; manned by undocumented immigrants, ex-cons, and kids from the projects; and frequented by New Yorkers looking to move uptown for more space and lower rent, and who needed to validate their newfound appreciation for the terra incognita above Central Park. If Frederick Douglass Boulevard were the neck connecting known Manhattan territory and the feared terrain above it, Culture was certainly the mouth that opened and closed, the inlet and outlet of hipness during my time there. And my job as hostess was not dissimilar to being an ambassador. I campaigned not only for the plates of shrimp and cheese grits or the cups of tall foam, but also for the neighborhood's livability and safety. The building that housed us scraped around a row of padlocked brownstones. It was up to me to make that an unknown detail of our whereabouts.

The woman reading Sunday Styles waved me over. She asked for another napkin and leaned over to whisper, "You live here, yes?"

"Two blocks north and a block east. Love it here." That's all I had to say, standing neck-long in my zebra-print dress with my armful of brunch menus and a clipboard, like a secretary waiting beside her boss's desk. Many guests asked me the same question, sometimes less directly and sometimes more, and always I answered with only praise for the area and for our staff. I named our front-of-the-house and back-of-the-house people, sharing a tidbit about each of them: their talents, hobbies, affiliations. About my European coworkers, I shared not only their country of origin but also their city of birth—Vienna, Copenhagen, Berlin. The pre-2010s were a very Europhilic time. Just think of the shows and movies and books we consumed, most of them just a spin-off of *Globe Trekker* and the *Before Sunrise* film series. Prague was hot, too. Everyone spoke of it, wrote about it, and dressed in monotone turtlenecks that gave off the same broody vibe as our mental images of the Czech city. Look nice, be nice, emphasize our Euro-ness. That was the job, though the last phrase was unspoken.

I noted, depending on whom I was talking to and my assessment of their knowledge of Southeast Asian geography, my country of origin *or* my city of birth. It was a toss-up: about half of our customers knew that Manila was the capital of the Philippines.

Every interaction at Culture between customer and staff, and between coworkers, revealed an interesting aspect of Harlem, of how we navigated these spaces as immigrants, as New Yorkers of color. A few weeks into my new job, we had a few idlers come in with a deck of cards on a slow day. They sipped, as opposed to drank, their coffee. I walked over to their two-top table to tell them that O, who was flipping omelets in the kitchen, was a genius at cards and chess, but I never mentioned where he might have played many rounds of poker and rummy. They said they'd love to come back when he's not busy, and even walked to the kitchen to wave goodbye to him as they were leaving.

At break time, I told Devonte to follow me outside, where I had set up my laptop on a patio table. I logged on to the café's Wi-Fi and pulled up a free GED test prep for him to browse. I told him I'd bring the laptop with me on our overlapping shifts, and that he could use it to review and register for the test. Ever coy and quiet, he just smirked and didn't say anything, until I said I was going back inside to make myself an iced tea.

"Yo, you can't leave this out here with me," he said. "They gonna think I stole it."

I sat with him until our break was over and assured him again that he could use my computer anytime. While he scrolled up and down and read practice questions, I thought of how every exchange, every situation, could become a death trap for him—even a fifteen-minute window of time to sit down with an electronic device not atypical at cafés.

As Devonte and I walked back inside, I heard the customers at the three-top table by the chalkboard menu make pleased sounds over the fingerling potatoes and baked eggs. I said, "E. J. is the culinary master behind it." But of course, E. J. also cooked Spam and eggs and fried chicken for his gang mates. He'd introduced me to them one Friday evening as I was counting tips and closing the register. E. J. walked in, followed by six or seven guys. He sidled up to the register, and said, "How you doin'?" I thought, *This is it,* having heard from my next-door neighbor Marcella that Harlem gang initiations sometimes involved heckling, harassing, or even raping chicks they came across on a Harlem street.

"Just counting my tips. Slow night," I said without a pause between *tips* and *slow.*

He leered and turned around to his friends ever so slowly, his eyes lagging to stay pinned on me as his neck rotated away. I thought of reaching back to the bar sink for a knife. But he spoke. "Y'all, nobody touch her. We watch her. Y'all cool?" He leaned in toward me and thanked me for convincing Devonte to take the GED, and thanked me for praying for his little cousin who'd been taken by the Department of Social Services.

Mouth dry, I said, "Anytime, E. J."

I never spoke of the encounter, nor how I momentarily felt terrified of a colleague, not even to Sean.

Conduit, embassy—Culture offered more than just new soul food and caffeine. It gave gentrifiers a spot to dillydally before they entered upper-upper Manhattan, and it gave Harlemites downtown ameni-ties that were previously a subway ride or two away. And I, in that place of business, came to work three times a week thinking that I got paid twelve dollars per hour, plus shared tips, to moderate things said and unsaid and to rectify—in a wrap dress or flowy tunic, in my not-Black but not-White skin, and definitely with my pearly whites flashing across my face—what had been assumed or believed about the neighborhood. But it wasn't until an encounter just outside the café that I would understand the power my petite, Southeast Asian, twenty-something body held.

The Fall

Neja, Odilia, and I connected about fashion, the foods we missed from back home, and what it was like to code switch as polyglots. We all also had similar CD collections—house music mainly popular outside the United States. Their faces lit up when I told them that I had a brother back home who composed and arranged tribal world house, and I liked it when I didn't have to explain (in the form of humming and tapping) what the music subgenre sounded like. Sometimes we showed up for work fifteen minutes early so we could put earphones in each other's ears to share tunes we'd discovered that week. And most vital for our line of work, Neja and Odilia introduced me to my newfound love of espresso. They made my first cup of almond milk mocha.

But I spent the most time with Lukas outside of work, so much so that I felt it was right to check with my long-distance boyfriend to find out how he felt about it. But my boyfriend, a Southern boy I'd been dating since we met in Midtown three years prior, had no qualms about it because, well, he just generally did not have any qualms about anything. That's why I liked him.

Lukas and I related about German-language films, what we liked and didn't like about Americans (My gosh, the constant apologizing!), and our passion for the arts. We talked about how we hoped to make it—me as a writer, and he as an actor—without legal, long-term resident status. We wondered if either of us would be lauded enough in our fields that we would be awarded O-1 visas, which are given to internationals with exceptional achievements in entertainment, science, math, or the arts. Lukas was slender but cut. You wouldn't fear him if you saw him, unlike Sean, who had to soften his brusqueness with dandyish outfits and friendly grins, but you also wouldn't put it past Lukas to break someone's leg or neck should he be provoked. And, like the two other Viennese people I'd met at the time, he had the utmost courtesy. He always walked me home or checked that I made it to my apartment door.

What he and I didn't realize was that on our walks, someone was watching us. I learned this on my way to work one morning. I had my earphones on and bobbed my head along to the track blaring from my portable MP3 player, when a man in a camo utility jacket jumped in my path and started spewing words at my face. I couldn't hear what he was saying, but I could make out that he was yelling, so I moved to the other side of the sidewalk and started walking faster. He caught up with me and kept yelling, his face so close to my own I could feel his breath on my nose in the cold late-October air. I walked even faster. But he kept with my pace. I pulled my earphones off and heard him say, "Café!"

"What?" I yelled back.

"CAFÉ! You work at the café!"

"I do, but why are you yelling at me?"

"You got your earphones on."

"You're scaring me."

He stepped back. "Scaring you? Wow." He started shaking his head frantically. "Is that why you always have to be walked home by your White boyfriend, huh?"

"He's not—my boyfriend doesn't even live—leave me alone!"

"'Cause I scare you, huh, you racist bitch!"

Taken aback by his comment, I thought of running away. But I did not want to affirm what he said or what he thought I just said, so I excused myself and said under my breath that I was late for work and ambled away. I arrived at Culture still so shaken by the encounter that I forgot to put my apron on and had to be reminded about it by Sean. He pulled me to the other side of the espresso machine and asked if I was okay. I nodded. He persisted. I finally told him that I had a strange encounter with someone on the street, but I relayed the story vaguely. I didn't say what was said to me, nor did I mention feeling the man's hot breath on my face. Sean suggested I take an extra ten minutes to prepare for work, that I take a breather under the awning outside.

I stood leaning against the floor-to-ceiling window, my rear resting on the ledge. Had I been a smoker, I would've been smoking. Instead I puffed out heavy breaths. As I was just calming down, my heart began to pound again. I saw him. He walked into the café wearing the same camo jacket and the same aggravated look on his face. He had more of a hunch, though, more of a swagger to his walk. I knew he didn't see me standing outside because a crowd of diners were putting on their outerwear as they exited—a shield of arms and coats.

I waited a couple of minutes before following him in, until he had situated himself in a window seat. I picked up my clipboard, menus, and pitcher, walked to his table, and filled his glass. I set a menu down in front of him but kept my eyes on my shoes. I said, softly, "Neja will be your server today."

He tried to look amused.

I seated other guests. My conversations started slow, and some regulars asked if I was okay. "Long day but I'm okay," I said with an obligatory grin. I cleared and turned several tables, refilled my pitchers with water from the tap, and topped off guests' glasses. I made a counterclockwise round of the tables, his at one o'clock, my last stop. A couple of customers away, I saw that his glass was full. A relief, I thought. I headed toward the register for some paper towels to wipe greasy menus with, but Neja grabbed my shoulder from behind and said, nodding toward my adversary, "Table over there wants you."

I asked what the guest needed, and she said that the man requested that I assist him with a complaint. I looked around for Sean, but I remembered that he was interviewing a prospective employee outside the café. "Go, babe, he's waiting," Neja said.

I walked over. "Anything I can help you with, sir?"

"Soy milk."

"Excuse me?"

"I changed my mind. I don't want half-and-half."

I returned with a stainless steel pitcher of soy milk. He shook his head as he pressed his tongue against the inside of his cheek.

I controlled my sigh and slipped my hands into my apron pockets. "Anything else I can help you with?"

"Changed my mind again. I'll take the dairy. Just wanted to make sure that you realized Black people drank soy milk, too. Milk substitutes aren't just for White people."

I formed fists in my apron pockets. I considered saying that I didn't think soy milk was just for White people, or that I wasn't White but liked almond milk in my lattes. But I remained diplomatic. I tipped my head, took the soy milk back to the kitchen, and brought out a fresh pitcher of half-and-half. When I came back out of the kitchen, Neja was sliding into the window seat to sit next to the man. They giggled.

I set the cream down and raised a brow.

He reached his hand forward, as if to shake mine, and said, "My name's Mo."

I didn't shake his hand. "What's going on?"

Neja put an arm around him and said, "Mo and I just thought it would be funny to give you a reason to frown." She high-fived Mo and complimented him on his acting skills.

He said, "I was so convincing, I fuckin' scared the shit outta this chick."

My eyes narrowed.

Neja turned back to me and said that she was getting tired of seeing me smile and be nice to everyone all the time. "So fuckin' Filipino." She and Mo snickered in a way that made them wheeze.

I pulled a rag out of my apron pocket and threw it onto the table. "Your jokes. You clean."

"Babe!" she called out as I walked back into the kitchen. "We're just playin', babe!"

I pushed through the rest of my shift unobtrusively, avoiding eye contact with Neja and the rest of the staff; I wasn't sure who else was in on the joke. Sean didn't seem to notice the stiff mood that afternoon because he was giving the new hire a tour of the kitchen and basement storage. After the last diners left, he called us all for a family meeting and introduced Manuel, the new dishwasher. Manuel was to alternate shifts with Devonte, now that Devonte was studying for the GED. Sean asked us to introduce ourselves to Manuel, and I went last, after everybody else had shuffled away from the kitchen and begun packing up their stuff. I walked over to Manuel, who stood shyly by the kitchen sink, and told him my name and that I was the hostess at the café. He asked me if I spoke Spanish, and I said, "Más o menos." He asked if anybody else did, and I shrugged.

"Ayúdame, okay?" he said with a clownish look on his face.

I told him that he would be fine, that his job was pretty straightforward. I made a circling motion with my hand to look like I was washing a plate. I gave him a thumbs-up, which he mirrored back to me. Then I warned him about Neja and her tricks. "Ten cuidado," I said as I led his eyes with my own toward Neja. "Con la rubia danesa."

Manuel braced himself and pretended to shiver, his way of saying *cold*. Since Neja had her biases against Filipinos, I did not put it past her to have biases against Mexicans or Latinos or anyone, really. And, it turned out, Manuel and I had our own feelings toward Danes.

"Por supuesto. Frío," he said.

And I said, "Hielo."

Two things changed that night: I began doubting Neja's efforts to be friends—her music recommendations, the way she called me and Odilia *babe*, and how she squeezed between me and Lukas and put her arms around us anytime we stood next to each other. I didn't offer her anything more than a sarcastic smile when she did these things, but I also tried not to stir whatever rancor she harbored against me or my people. I started to decline Lukas's offers to walk me home and—this was my white lie—blamed it on the long-distance boyfriend. But, again with his Viennese sense of courtesy, he did not ask questions, did not say that the boyfriend was foolish, and did not defend the fact that he was merely being nice and nothing more. I missed Lukas on my walks home, mostly because I lost someone to talk to about being an artist *and* an undocumented. While my boyfriend and I could talk for hours on the phone, and while he and I could not have been more alike in what made us happy, sad, proud, or embarrassed, my boyfriend was born in America to property- and land-owning White evangelicals. He did not understand, even if he wanted to, what it was like to live in constant hypervigilance.

I also began to doubt what I was doing there—at Café Culture and in Harlem. To one group of people—our guests—my smile was welcoming, engaging, and comforting. To be pleasing, if not overly pleasing, was to fulfill my duties, to assuage whatever fears or apprehension people brought with them from downtown. To another group, my eagerness to delight, entertain, connect—whatever I thought was my job description at Culture and *for* culture—was an annoyance, an unwelcome practice, an intrusion. I was hailing in a new population formerly indifferent to the geography, sociology, economy, *humanity* of the place, while I wasn't even so sure of how altruistic their motives were for venturing north: Did they even care about the longtime residents? There, too, was Neja, to whom my hospitality was grating, and who perhaps even fostered resentment toward my nationality and culture.

Neja's prank marked my third month at the café. The beginning of my fourth was the start of a string of holidays. All was a frenzy. The busyness made for more of a come-and-go customer experience, with guests calling in orders of pumpkin-spice mochas or extra-shot espressos and running out the door. Weekend brunch, too, became automatically chatty even without my help. It was boisterous because everyone was glued to their iPhones and willing to comment on what their phones said about the potentially historic presidential race. I did not have to initiate "meet your neighbor," which meant Neja didn't have as many opportunities to criticize me.

And then there was November 4, 2008. I called my boyfriend and used my precious calling minutes to tell him that Obama had won. We celebrated by screaming into our phones. I ran out my door and found my neighbor, Marcella, smoking on the fire escape and petting her Chihuahua, Simba.

"You watchin' this, baby girl?" she said in her jazzy voice. Marcella used to sing jingles for Campbell's soup commercials and appear in episodes of *Ghostwriter*. She was also one of the longtime residents at our building, Graham Court, and was able to still live there because of rent control. My apartment used to be part of her apartment, but the landlord divided the space to bank on the influx of new renters.

"I'm running downstairs to see it."

"Baby girl, I've been Black all my life and been in Harlem a long time, and this might be the happiest I've ever seen it."

We smiled at each other. "You coming downstairs?"

"Nah," she said. "It'll only last for a short while. I'm so slow, it'll be over by the time I get there."

I wondered what she meant by *it*, but only briefly, because I was excited about joining whatever was going on outside.

"You still there?" my boyfriend said on the phone. He asked why I was panting, and I told him that the elevator was broken again and I was running down the steps from my fifth-floor apartment and out onto the street. When I got to the building gate on Adam Clayton Powell Junior Boulevard and 116th Street, I could not believe my eyes. A parade as thick as the boulevard marched uptown. I could hear the celebrations from inside my apartment, but I had not realized how many Harlemites would be out on the street, singing, dancing, and crying as they chanted, "Yes, we can!" Parents pushed their kids in strollers or carried them on their shoulders. Cooks and servers abandoned their stations and dashed toward the Apollo Theater in their aprons, some still holding their black check folders. Grandmothers wobbled out of buildings with their walkers. One said as she struggled down three cinder block steps, "Oh, Lord, I have waited. I have waited so long." That was when I cried.

"I wish you could see this," I told my boyfriend on the phone. "Everyone is so happy."

"Describe it to me," he said.

Like a dispatcher detailing a newsworthy scene, I described what I saw: people hugging, men in suits holding Bibles and men in suits holding briefcases shaking each other's hands, women weeping, teen-agers holding up Obama campaign posters and cloths spray-painted with the words *HOPE* and *CHANGE*, drummers banging on African drums. "You have to hear it," I said and held my phone above my head like an antenna channeling all the good Harlem energy to wherever he was in South Carolina. "So beautiful," I said of the people and their democracy.

And I thought, *So fragile.*

The Winter It All Went Down

"Well, shit," Sean said when we got to the door. It was unlocked, even though he was certain he had locked it the night before. Shaking his head, he walked over to the counter and found what he had already guessed: a missing cash register. He scratched an eyebrow and told me to start wrapping silverware in napkins. "I'll call the cops and do the talkin'."

A police officer came, and we kept the "Closed" sign on the door for an hour longer. He asked Sean to list broken or missing items and how much cash was in the register. He also asked who else had a key. In what I considered was his way of protecting *all* of us, especially those of us who weren't favored by authorities or the law, Sean said, "Everyone's got a key." In reality, only the cooks, Sean, and Odilia had keys. He told the officer that the register had less than a hundred dollars because he had made a deposit to the bank the previous afternoon, and that it wasn't necessary to open an investigation or press charges.

"So why'd you call us?" the cop said.

"Just thought it'd be good to make the call. But no real harm done, officer. Thank you."

The cop slapped his pocket notebook closed, clearly irked, and walked out. Sean followed him out the door to say another thanks, saluted the officer, and flipped the door sign to "Open" as he came back in.

"Not worth it. Never is," he said. "Don't even know why I called." He sulked as he straightened the café. I felt how sorry he was not just for the theft, but for having reported it. It was pure reflex to call. But somewhere between dialing and the cop asking questions, I think Sean realized that having authorities at Culture could lead to questions upon questions, to consequences not worth the eighty or so dollars in the register. Eighty dollars, or even a hundred or two hundred, wasn't worth compromising the safety of the two guys we both suspected had committed the crime. It also wasn't worth the safety of those of us working off the books.

Sean made two calls that morning, one to fire O and the other to fire E. J. I heard him end both calls with, "Didn't have to be this way, man. Doin' it for everybody else."

With no cooks, we served only drinks and baked goods that day. Over the next few days, Sean and Odilia worked in the kitchen, often overcooking the food. The shrimp that went with the grits were rubbery. The baked eggs, too. They let the red-velvet batter stay too long in the waffle maker, so that the waffles came out crunchy instead of fluffy. Salads were their saving grace. So I recommended salads to all my guests.

Thank God that Sean hired two new cooks within a few days—there was never a shortage of back-of-the-house help in New York, especially among the undocumented. First to train was a stocky thirty-something-year-old Irish-Englishman from what he described as a "run-down part of London." His accent was not like the British accents I heard on television, and his clothes looked like they used to fit him, as though he'd been even bigger at one point: tight around the shoulders but loose everywhere else. He had cinched his pants with a belt, even though he wore them to ride low around his hips. When introduced to Lukas and me, he just said, "Pleasure. Damien."

When I tried to make conversation and asked how long he'd been in the States, he murmured, "Eight months."

When I asked if he had family or friends in New York, he pulled out his flip phone and showed me a picture of a little girl with braids. I assumed that she was why he came to New York, and why, like the rest of us, he'd overstayed his visa.

Damien worked quietly, always with a scowl. I avoided him when I could, because he always looked like he was about to blow but was keeping all the steam in. I skirted around the espresso machine as opposed to walking through the small space between his stove and the sink. Manuel stood on the same two-foot square to avoid getting in Damien's way, stacking his dishes high so he didn't have to stretch them along Damien's countertop. Lukas knew to relay each special order accurately and clearly, to avoid having to send a plate back to the kitchen. The three of us felt that although Damien came off as unfriendly, he was actually just hurting.

During breaks, or when Damien clocked out before us, the three of us whispered our hunches to each other. Manuel thought that perhaps, like him, the Irish-Englishman carried a mix of sadness and guilt that was not unrelated to having to cross borders for his little girl. We understood. While we did fear crossing him and causing him to finally lash out, we did not take his surliness personally. Neja, however, did not appreciate his lack of warmth. She liked to be indulged with praise, especially by guests, and generously gave compliments herself—to the point of bootlicking. She was always touching our guests, putting her hands on their shoulders or sometimes even giving them a back rub after she set down their plates. She took Damien's silence as a slight against her outlandish and needy ways. She could not be pleased. She reminded me of an expression we had in the Philippines: Sala sa init, sala sa lamig, or "people around whom you cannot be warm, cannot be cold." They are as fickle as the weather. Once, Neja wrote *FAT* on an order slip she passed across the counter to Damien. "I mean the sauce. It needs more fat, like bacon grease or something." But we all knew she was trying to insult him. Damien just put his earphones on and kept his head down while making a fattier, thicker roux.

The second cook Sean hired could not have contrasted Damien more. His name was Cheikh, and he was a native of Senegal who resided on my street—West 116th, also known as Le Petit Senegal. Cheikh came to his interview in a sunburst-yellow kaftan and to his first day of training in an orange one. He talked on his phone all day using a Bluetooth accessory, which meant that sometimes I wasn't sure if he was giving me instructions or if he was talking to his cousin in New Jersey. When he did talk to me to ask me about my father and my sister and my brother and my long-distance boyfriend and my studies, I had to interrupt him and tell him that I had to go back to my station by the door. But he rattled on anyway even as I walked away. He had the gift of gab and was not afraid to use it, not even around Damien, who lived in an invisible cocoon of ennui and ire.

Their shifts overlapped during brunch hours, when the café was at its busiest. Cheikh's hand gestures and exaggerated movements overtook the five-foot stretch of space behind the stove. When he flipped omelets, we could hear the swish of his sleeve and the slapping sound the omelet made when it landed on the sizzling pan. Needless to say, he crowded the kitchen, and poor Damien had to work with a mise en place arranged on a flat surface no bigger than a sheet of printing paper.

"Obnoxious, mate," Damien finally said one day.

We all stopped what we were doing. Even Sean was afraid to make a sound.

Cheikh pulled his Bluetooth off his ear and slipped it into his apron pocket. "What you say, porky?"

The kitchen filled with a collective gasp. Sean looked to me and Odilia. With jaws dropped, we stared back at him, speechless. "Lukas!" I said. He rushed to get between Damien and Cheikh, who were both about half a foot taller than he, and pressed his palms against each of their chests. I followed suit, grabbed Cheikh by the arm, and pulled him toward the espresso machine. I said, "Cheikh, have I told you about my new business idea?" He was always interested in business ideas. He showed me a notebook of them once: pages of doodles and scribbles for what he called "the next big American thing." I made up a concept for unlimited cell phone minutes and told him that he should walk to the T-Mobile store on West 125th Street to propose the idea. "Imagine, my friend, no more scratch-off cards or running out of minutes. You pay a monthly fee and talk all you want!" My yakking bought Sean time to get over to Damien, who was breathing heavily and balling a fist, and escort him outside to stand under the awning and cool off.

Cheikh pointed his finger at me, then wagged it. He said, "Clever girl."

"*Pfft*," Neja fussed as she set a tray of glasses down by Manuel and the sink. "Drama schrama."

My next shift was not until a few weekdays later. Sean had sent text messages to the waitstaff about shift rotations: Damien and Cheikh were no longer to overlap shifts, and Odilia and Sean were to do prep for them during brunch service. He promoted me, or so he put it, from hostess to floor manager, to seat guests, rectify front-of-the-house mistakes, handle complaints, and liaise between the kitchen and the floor. He and Odilia would take care of back-of-the-house operations and food faux pas. This, he said, would allow for a smoother service and a calmer kitchen. Prepared for, and quite proud of, my advancing in the food-and-bev industry, I marched two blocks south and one avenue west from my apartment sporting a new trench coat and red lipstick.

But I arrived outside a café where outdoor seats had not been unstacked nor unchained from the metal slide-down door. The lights inside were turned on but dimmed, as if the café were getting ready for dinner service or a live music event. I saw Sean on one of the communal tables, his head in his hands, sitting stricken as men with walkie-talkies searched the café. Lukas appeared from around the corner and stopped. I glared at him and he understood. He walked backward, back around the corner and behind the building. A man with a walkie-talkie stepped through the open door and said, "Can I help you, miss?"

"Coffee," I said, nervous about saying anything else or anything more.

"Excuse me?" the man said.

"Miss, we're closed today. Sorry," Sean said from where he was sitting. He stood up and walked to the door. He waved me away, then formed one hand into the shape of a telephone. "I apologize, but please come back soon."

I turned around and headed south toward Lukas's apartment. I found him crouched on a Harlem stoop, reading a message on his phone. It reminded me that Sean had gestured for me to do the same. I pulled out my phone and read his message: INS GOT DAMIEN. My neck stiffened and my throat tightened. I had almost walked into a scene full of immigration officers. Had Sean not had the presence of mind to stop me from entering, they would've had the chance to ask if I worked there. They would have asked for an ID. I could have been taken. Lukas and Odilia and Manuel and Cheikh and Neja, too. But Odilia was off that week to see her brother. Cheikh now only worked afternoon or evening shifts. Manuel always arrived slightly later than the waitstaff. But Neja—where was she? Why was she not on her way to work? Why had Lukas and I not run into her yet? She lived the same distance from Culture as I did.

"That bitch!"

"Shh!" Lukas tried to shush me. "They might come here."

"Go home, Lukas. Stay home and don't answer calls from Neja." I made a detour toward home, several blocks south, then east, then back north and west. I looped around to touch the upper perimeter of Central Park where people jogged or had set out blankets for picnics. I semicircled up then over to Spanish Harlem, where Manuel lived and where I hoped to run into him. Since I did not have his phone number, I couldn't warn him of the presence of authorities at the café. Back on West 116th, I crossed the width of Lenox Avenue and walked down Le Petit Senegal, hoping again that I'd run into a coworker who needed to know that our place had just been raided. That someone had tipped. *Ten cuidado,* I thought, *con la rubia danesa.*

Sean called us to a family meeting the following morning. We each fixed a drink before sitting around the communal tables. The group consisted of Sean, all four part-time staff, and the six of us who'd just evaded deportation. Sean explained what had happened the morning before, that someone had tipped the INS about Damien and his whereabouts, and that the authorities arrived at the café just minutes after Sean and Damien let themselves in. He said that the authorities seemed to know what time the cooks arrived, which meant the rat knew our routine.

"Cheikh was mad at him," Neja said.

"Ey, no!" Cheikh said. "Shut your fat mouth, snowflake!"

Neja and Cheikh went back and forth, using slurs from many languages:

"African ass!"

"Pute!"

"Moslem terrorist!"

"Gypsy whore!"

"Monkey!"

"Toubab bitch!"

"Dit svin!"

"Salope!"

"Enough!" Sean said. He lectured us as loudly as he could, trying to speak over Neja's and Cheikh's grunting and huffing. He said that it was now up to us whether to stay or leave, that Culture was definitely on immigration services' radar. We could go on as usual, as if nothing had happened, as if nothing could affect us—and maybe the authorities wouldn't suspect more. Or we could all quit and he could shake up his roster, maybe hire only citizens and permanent residents for six months or so, and hire us all back when things mellowed. "Let me know by the end of the week."

"Sean, this is totally unfair!" I said. "We all know who did it! We all know who wasn't here when it happened!"

"Are you blaming me?" Neja said.

"Did I say your name? Are you guilty?"

"Oh, is Cheikh your boyfriend now, too?"

"Neja!" Sean bellowed. His deepened voice made the communal table rumble under us. We sat silently and nervously for a moment before he spoke again. "None of this goes on your Facebook, we clear?"

Spring Forward

Nina and I pretend that we are more athletic than we are and try to jog around the Central Park reservoir. We do not make it halfway, not even a quarter way, around the body of water before we stop at an ice-cream cart. Nina *is* springtime: golden hair; orange long-sleeve shirt; moss-green stretchy pants; bright and peppy and comfortable. She chats with the vendor and with me. She chirps away like a morning bird. I unwrap my rocket-shaped Popsicle.

It is April and the city has begun to thaw, but the Popsicle is still too cold for my teeth. I let it decrystalize in the sun and watch the freezer frost melt and give way to the bright red underneath.

"Hey, are you listening? What did you decide?" Nina asks as she plops onto the grass.

I sit down next to her. "Decide what?"

She berates me with reasons to quit my job. I lick the Popsicle.

"Don't you *care*?" she says.

I don't give her an answer until I finish my treat. I lick my lips and wipe them with my pullover sleeve, and I ask her what she thinks I'll be doing when we graduate. I tell her that with my recent promotion at Culture, it would be hard to walk away. Undocumented people cannot apply for most jobs, much less get promoted, much less feel seen. At the café, I have employment, I have and will continue to move up, and, as is my job description, my face is the face of the place. People see me. People know me. Some regulars even notice when I've added a brooch to an old blazer or if I've switched bronzers. Working there, I can earn a living and talk books, art, fashion, history—all the things I've gone to school for. Books, art, fashion, history—were these not the things I had been erased from once I was deemed unfit to be a protected member of a state? Don't we call them *the humanities* because they are supposedly what make us human, or acceptably human? Was being learned or worldly or talented not the currency that often bought me eye contact and first-name basis with guests and classmates and teachers? Outside of Culture, I'd be lucky if I could get another off-the-books job that will permit me to lavish myself with such seemingly cultured conversations. At Café Culture, I feel like I am a part of modern American history—and is that not somewhat the antithesis of being called undocumented? When I came to America as a minor and was denied the right to stay, did they not teach me to believe that I was nothing?

Nina parts her lips a few times in an effort to respond. "I didn't . . . know."

"I know you didn't know," I say, but not to console her. I tell her that no citizen, left wing or right wing, really knows the nothingness, the non-being, undocumented young adults constantly live with and anticipate. Legal residents might come close to the knowledge of it, but they have the safety of an approved identity—accepted humanity—on a laminated card.

She apologizes again, and I am reminded of how Lukas mocks Americans for their constant apologizing. I wonder how sorry Nina really is.

"I'm really sorry, really." Nina begins to cry.

"Oh, good god," I say and put an arm around her. "Nina, please. We're in America. We're bound to hurt each other's feelings."

We walk back to Harlem and don't speak all the way home. I think the entire way, *Who is more delicate—me, her, or this place?* And I think, too, *Who is allowed this fragility?*

That Summer and the Summer After

Summer greets us the weekend after graduation, and I launch myself into it with packed bags and a granny cart full of housewares. The recession has hit Manhattan hard and nobody can find a job, not even Nina. My longtime and long-distance boyfriend has been denied by multiple companies and graduate programs in the city due to lack of funding and an overload of applicants. With a poor job market, everyone decides to go back to school to wait out the economic downturn. The only open door is a graduate degree and stipend that awaits my boyfriend all the way in Georgia, for which he relocates, and for which I follow him and give up my New York City dreams.

Marcella warns me in the elevator about moving south. "Baby girl, you ain't Black but you ain't White. I can't tell you not to go to Georgia or Cockalina or wherever your bitty self needs to go, but don't say I didn't warn you."

I tell her that I will be okay.

"If they upset or hurt you, you call me, and Simba and I will come runnin' and bitin'."

The elevator door opens, and we flood our floor with laughter. She begins to sing "Leaving on a Jet Plane," and I say, "Actually, I'm taking a train. TSA, remember?"

"Baby girl, I didn't write the song!" She pulls me to her and hugs me, and my face squishes into her bosom, and I feel her voice vibrate out of her as she continues to sing. As she belts it out, I say a silent prayer, hoping that she'll never be kicked out of our beloved building, that she'll be able to keep flooding our floor, elevator, and lobby with her laughter and voice.

By late June, Café Culture struggles to pay the rent bill. Sean is forced to thin out the staff. He first asks Cheikh to turn in his apron. Cheikh's loudness transforms into utter disregard for staff and guests. I give my two weeks' notice. Lukas moves to California. Odilia gets married and soon after gets pregnant. Devonte gets his GED, goes to culinary school, and later on becomes a sous-chef in a Bravo reality TV show. Neja transfers to a speakeasy funded by the same investors who back the café, and her attitude and tricks fit the environment really well. Only Manuel and Sean stay. They will stay until the café closes in 2011.

A year after graduation, in 2010, I will return to New York as a young bride and walk down a gravel path to a fountain in Central Park. I will become a permanent resident. Seven years after, I will take my naturalization exam and my oath of citizenship. I will learn the Pledge of Allegiance and "The Star-Spangled Banner." But before that, in front of that fountain, I will stand in the sun in a white dress, say "I do," and at the ceremony's closing, look north to Harlem and breathe in. I will smell the purple flowers in my hands, but I will smell, too, if only from memory, the aroma of coffee.

Carefree White Girls,
Careful Brown Girls

If I were a White girl, I'd want to be the kind that's just like K. L.

She used to roll out of bed just before noon after a night at Surf Bar and Sand Dollar Social Club, mount her longboard onto the Jeep, drive to the Washout, and ride Carolina's biggest waves until the northeast groundswell rested. Then she was off to work to deliver drugs. She picked up packages from some beach shack or surf shop, from a frat boy at the dunes on Folly Beach—the same beach where the best female surfers from the East Coast and Puerto Rico gather every year in June for the Folly Beach Wahine Classic, a surf competition that caters only to women and girls. Wahine: Hawaiian for *woman*.

But it was on another Charleston beach, on another stretch of dunes, where she and I met. She was at Isle of Palms to teach surf lessons, and I was there to learn, to redevelop my core strength after giving birth, and to do something I'd always wanted to do before it was too late—before motherhood took over every part of me and clouded out time for things that, at this point, might have seemed superfluous. There was also, always, the question of money. This class was free, as the vinyl sign on the tent said.

"I'm a mom, too," she said. "I'm K. L." She recognized my anxious energy and despite it, she pulled me into hers. We started talking right there, right before the roaring ocean, a blonde chick and a Filipina, because I had a whimpering baby on my hip and she had a whining preteen at her side, and we both knew we weren't spending our day at the beach with men today. Today was wahine time.

"You're one of the teachers?" I said, exhaling the salty air I had gulped in, relieved that I wouldn't have to lie on some man's board and receive instructions from him, relieved that I wouldn't have to slide in and out of the water in a swimsuit with a man watching my every move, relieved that this first time wouldn't be a trigger, that it wouldn't remind me of every time I've lain next to or under a man, confused, unwilling, stock-still. She curled her three middle fingers in and winged out her thumb and pinkie, the surfer hand sign for *hang loose*, and shook her hand forth and back between us, to say without speaking, *You and me*. She wore elastic bands on both wrists, so many that they looked like a cuff. She wore them, a string bikini, and nothing else, but even with so little on, I could sense her style. She reminded me of the protagonists from my favorite movie as a teen, *Blue Crush*—three young girls with no money but unlimited water-sports skills and beach-life flair.

"Where do I sign?"

K. L. handed me a waiver on a clipboard and told me who she and her group were. "We're Christian surfers who give free surf lessons—I guess you can say that many of us were saved by surfing."

This was the rehearsed part of her speech, the only line that I thought came from somewhere other than her natural edge and the part of her that I saw in me—that small but strong propensity for risk and for the surf I was eager to meet. She held my baby while I practiced my paddle on the sand. Her daughter taught my nephew, who was spending the summer with us and was also along for my lesson, how to pop up on a board. She took me out to the water, told me to paddle harder, to wait, to go catch that wave.

I fell off the board many times, sometimes swallowing water or inhaling it, but each time K. L. yelled, waist deep in the water and holding my baby, "Get back on the board! Do it again!" My sinuses stung from the saline, but every time I brushed my hand up to my nose and blew out salt water, she yelled, "It's just water!" She flung her hand toward the deep, as if to throw in a hook on a fishing line, and yelled again, "Go out there! Paddle!"

It was sundown soon after my first successful try at getting my feet on the board, and it was time for each of us to head home and make dinner, to do the dishes and laundry, to be Mom again, to think of the waves as we fell asleep. I closed my eyes thinking of what a good day it was, how accomplished I felt, and how much I liked K. L.

I emailed her the next morning and asked if she would like to come over for tea sometime, and she responded within an hour. When my phone buzzed, I sprang onto the couch to reach for it. I had never been this excited for a playdate or a mom date, because I had never met a White or Southern mom that I identified with as much as I did with K. L.

She came for tea the following week, and between the email and her knock on the door, I thought of all that I wanted to share with her, how I would get her to tell me her truth. Did our proclivity for dangerous sports (before surfing, I snowboarded, rappelled, open-water Jet Skied, snorkeled with orcas, bungee jumped, and played soccer so fiercely, I once headed a ball hard enough that I almost went blind in my right eye) not mean that we each had danced with danger, that we each had eluded harm by a hair, that the need for thrill was planted in us?

She sat down in front of the cup of tea I had made for her but never touched it, and instead sipped the protein smoothie she had brought with her. "I'm trying to be healthy," she said. "Health*ier*. Tryin' to take care of my body after years of neglecting it."

I watched her let the tea cool, her fingers teetering on the edge of the table, then twirling and fidgeting with a tuft of her sun-bleached hair. She wasn't like this at all in the water. I started to think that this was wrong—maybe I didn't really want to be her friend. I tried to think of something to say to ease us both, but she finally said, "Just ask what you want to ask."

I had interviewed many people, in journalism school and for my first newspaper job in Georgia. But here I was, taking a moment before asking, "Who were you before you were a surf instructor?"

She smiled at me, then looked away, out the window, her blue eyes shimmering in the light like the ocean. She opened her mouth but paused. I thought that she was trying to decide whether to give me the truth or her rehearsed lines, so I said, "I'll tell you mine after."

She smiled again but kept her eyes off me, and didn't look at me until she finished her story. She began, "I was a drug delivery girl. I transported coke from the city to the beach and back, and sometimes to other places between here and New York." During our surf lesson, I had told her that I moved from New York, so I knew she was telling me this last detail to circle it back to me—to make sure I'd tell her *my* story.

"Was it always cocaine?" I said.

"Coke, Ecstasy, Xanax . . . whatever they pressed in their home labs, whatever they put in my beach bag, whatever I could hide in my bikini bottoms or board shorts."

"How'd you get into it?"

She told me that she was just a local surfer girl, a betty, a cute blonde who didn't want to go to college. She wanted to surf instead, to be like those locals who lived simply, had enough money for rent, food, and board wax; who waited tables at night and woke up to shred the gnar. It was going well until the beach and the city grew in popularity and the price of everything went up.

She had tried coke just for the heck of it, because all the kids were doing it, but when an ex-boyfriend asked if she wanted to make money from it, she said yes. He hooked her up with a friend and the friend's boss, and the next time she mounted her board onto the Jeep, she was loading a backpack of goods, too. They also gave her some to keep.

She drove into historic downtown and up and down the coast high, euphoric, but most importantly, immune to getting caught.

"It was a gig, a job, then a lifestyle."

When I asked if she ever got caught, she said that she was never stopped nor pulled over. Not once did anyone suspect that she had something other than sunscreen in her waterproof sack. "Nobody will stop a young blonde girl, that's the truth," she said, almost bragging, as she tousled the tips of her hair. She mussed up her hair and twisted it, took an elastic band from her wrist with her teeth, and snapped it around the flimsy bun. With her face and chin still pointed toward the window, she looked at me out of the corner of her eye and said, "We just get away with things, you know?" Unhappy with how she had just fixed her hair, she let it down again, let it bounce to her shoulders, and gathered it on one side. This was when I grew angry with her, when I wanted to scrap our week-old friendship. I forced a grin.

"You're right," I said. "I've never transported drugs, never even done drugs, but I've been stopped and ID'd at all sorts of places."

She finally glanced away from the window and gazed at me. "Your turn," she said.

"I was undocumented for eight years." Now I was the one looking away. "If you wanna know what that's like, just think the opposite of your story. I had to live as quietly as possible, be low-key at all times, even though I'd never committed a crime. I've never shoplifted or vandalized, not even as a teen. I couldn't travel by plane or Amtrak, couldn't even order a margarita without making up a whole lie about forgetting my ID at home. If there was a checkpoint at a subway stop, I'd walk home. I was in perpetual hiding."

I told her that if I said the wrong thing or looked at a guard or a cop the wrong way, I could attract the wrong kind of attention, get ID'd and interrogated, get sent to a detention center, or get deported. I said that in college, when I applied for paid internships, despite my grades and writing knowledge, I got turned down semester after semester because I couldn't fill out a W-9. Instead I accepted unpaid research or marketing positions or internships that didn't fulfill university credits.

I glanced at K. L. to see if she displayed any discomfort, any concern. But there she was, still playing with her hair and the elastics on her wrists, as if comfortably listening to a podcast. She caught me looking at her and said, "Sorry, go on." I dug into my memory for stories that I thought she couldn't ignore, stories that would perhaps engulf her in the strain of my experiences. They went:

When my then boyfriend, now husband proposed to me, and we had to acquire a marriage license from city hall in New York, the clerk whispered to the other clerk, showed her my forms, and said, "Just a minute." When they returned, they were accompanied by a cop and the office director. They asked my fiancé to wait outside and to hold my phone and purse, took me to a back room behind the copiers, and interrogated me. They asked me how I entered the country from the Philippines, and I said through adoption.

They asked me why I was adopted at sixteen, when I was old enough to drive, and I said that I'd been asking the same thing all my life—why did no one rescue me sooner? They asked me how I became undocumented after being adopted, and I said that their laws said I was too old to receive naturalization benefits, and that it took too long for our lawyer and the judge to file and stamp the hundreds of pages of required documents. They asked me why I didn't have an entry for father of the bride in the marriage license application, and I said that my adoptive parent was a widow. You don't need a man to give a minor a chance at life.

Finally, and I knew it was coming, they asked, "Young lady, how can we be sure that you're not marrying this man as a mail-order bride?"

I immediately got up from the chair.

"Sit back down, young lady."

I didn't sit back down and they didn't let me out, not until I proved that I wasn't purchased into the country. When I said that my fiancé was a graduate student with no money to buy a wife, that I had plans of attending grad school myself, and that a friend of mine was to officiate the wedding, the clerk looked at her colleagues and shrugged. "Really?" I said. I held my hand out, pointed at my ring, and said that it was heirloom jewelry passed down from my fiancé's dying aunt. The clerk finally took my application fee and stamped my form.

"Congrats," the clerk said without a smile as she handed over the marriage license.

Half a year after the interrogation in Manhattan, I found myself defending my identity again—this time in Atlanta. I needed antibiotics for a urinary tract infection and the most convenient place to get the prescription was the CVS MinuteClinic. The nurse practitioner on shift that day was a low-voiced woman who looked up from her clipboard only when you didn't answer quickly enough. After asking for my symptoms, and if I made a habit of peeing after sex, she asked, "That guy outside, is he really your husband?"

I showed her my ring.

"That don't mean a thing, hon."

"We've been married a few months. He was my boyfriend of four years."

"You sure he didn't pick you out of many at the airport?" She was referring to Atlanta's reputation as one of the busiest ports for sex trafficking and mail-order brides. I told her again that all I needed was an antibiotic, thanked her for looking out for me, and reached out my hand for the pills. She handed me the bottle and said, "You girls just always conning people or people are conning you, is all."

One Christmas, a cashier wouldn't sell me Earl Grey tea and a bag of pretzels because I did not look like the name on my credit card. "You don't look like a Barnes to me. This ain't yours." I asked her if she was looking for a Romero or a Gomez or a Lee, and all she said was, "We experience a lot of theft during the holidays, miss."

I told K. L. these stories, and I waited for her to say something, maybe apologize for how easy she could get away with crime. But she said nothing. Instead, she got up and walked to the sink to empty her smoothie tumbler and rinse it. Then she walked over to the freezer for ice like she'd walked to it many times, like she'd been in that kitchen to cook or eat or laugh or cry, like she owned the one place that was mine. I was furious at her now, or I was furious at the idea of her, of who she represented: White women everywhere who could fluidly slip in and out of spaces, toy with danger, even give danger a name, call it a gig, a job, a lifestyle.

"You didn't drink your tea," I said.

She just shrugged, because she had that power, that privilege, too. In my culture, in Filipino culture, you don't turn down your host. You eat and drink what they serve you, and you don't stop consuming until they stop bringing you things.

I started hoping for the baby to wake up from her nap so I could retrieve her from the crib and make it seem like it was time for K. L. to leave. But the baby stayed asleep. *Must be the clouds,* I thought. A storm was rolling in, which meant that the baby was falling into a deeper sleep and also that K. L. would avoid driving in the downpour. When it rains hard in Charleston, our options are to stay indoors and wait out the chances of a flash flood, or ride the flood in a kayak or small boat. I tried to think of something that could make our time together bearable, but it turned out I didn't have to. K. L. sat back down at the table with me, poured the room temperature tea into her tumbler of ice, and took a sip.

"I'm not much of a hot tea kinda girl," she said and took a sip again. She looked around the quiet house, saw where I had propped a bedroom door slightly open so I could hear the baby. "Baby's sleeping well, that's good. It's good to get a break."

"Yeah," I said, "motherhood's exhausting."

"It is, but having a daughter made me leave all that shit," she replied, and this was when I started listening again and believing that perhaps we had a common ground, because what I hadn't told her was that before I was adopted and became undocumented, I was living in an abusive home. When I got out of that home, I dealt with my previous trauma by self-injuring with needles and blades and by starving myself. I also slept around, even dated one of my professors. Nothing criminal, nothing that would hurt anybody else—just myself. The self-destructive habits ended when I found out I was pregnant. Like K. L., I let all that shit go when I became aware of a human growing inside me, swimming in my uterus, paddling in to join me in the come and go, to rescue me from drowning.

I looked up and she was in tears. She was crying into the tea. I reached for her hand to rub it and to tell her I was okay. And she said, "I'm not crying because of that. I'm crying because I thought you didn't like me. I don't have a lot of mom friends; I don't fit in that world."

"Neither do I."

We hugged and she went home, and we didn't see each other again except for a chance encounter at the beach the following summer. I bought a bike and cycling became my new hobby.

K. L. had told me what it was like to be her, and I had told her what it was like to be me. We couldn't have traded places even if we wanted to. We were born in the skin we were in, destined for our respective circumstances. I can only guess that there was guilt on her part that kept her away, an undertow of disdain on mine that discouraged me from reaching out again.

But still, I think of her, and I think of how I like her just fine. I even want to be her, live through her. I would like her even if she committed crime again, if she dared to go back to living so close to the edge. Why would it matter? She'd get away with it. Not me. I'm Brown, an immigrant. I'm forever clean. But she'd get away with danger. For both of us. For those parts of her and me that are just underneath, coming to a swell, like rip current backwashing from the shore, pulling to the deep.

Frenzied Woman

We had everything, then we had nothing. But I always had books and dance. This was my shorthand response to anyone who asked about my distant past, my pre-America. I say *distant* because the past happened in the Philippines, thousands of miles away, before the internet was as routine as checking the time or eating breakfast. The past had no online footprint. The past lived in recesses of my brain that had been walled off by art history facts, sewing techniques, and memorable World Cup plays. I had found a place for the past and there I kept it. The past was so distant, I could tell it like the summary of a fairy tale. Once upon a time, and I lived happily ever after. The shorthand was enough for years, for over a decade spent in New York, Georgia, and South Carolina, until I got a therapist who liked to read. She understood words, therefore she understood what I used them for, and how. My sentences were never too short nor too long for her—she liked to break down both. *When you said this, what did you mean?* An English major before she was a licensed trauma specialist, she saw my every anecdote as a scene, every verb a cause or effect, and every subject or object a motif.

Today's motif: *Tell me more about dance.*

What about it?

Tell me about it as if you were describing a ritual, something you religiously do. Your memories of it. You do *it religiously, don't you?*

I suppose. I've been dancing since I was three.

We start there. I was three. Or, more precisely, I was turning three and as I was turning numbers, growing, growing up, my baby brother died. I was going and he was stopping—these were the verbs I used for myself and him then. I'd been in ballet class that year because Mama thought first position could cure my pigeon-toe, and a tendu could fix my bowleggedness. The ballet did work, if we're talking about returns on my mother's investment. But it also worked in that it introduced me to a space that allowed for nothing but the movement of limbs, sashaying across floors, routines to go with the music, and outfits (always in aqua—en vogue at the time) to go with the routines. My body was not detested at the dance studio, like my mother detested my body, so long as I could plié and tiptoe to the beat. One, two, three. Two, two, three. Three, two, three. And four. I was lucky, too, to not have the kind of ballet teacher I saw in movies. My teacher, Ms. Anna, had a dimple on one cheek that always showed because she always smiled. My mother, on the other hand, stopped smiling when my brother stopped going. We buried my brother, his body, in our garden the night of my third birthday, and from that point on, my mother obsessed over what my body was doing—was it expanding, stretching, bowlegging, pigeon-toeing, making room for hives, scabs, and scars? She watched the end of every ballet class, when we would run through the entire routine learned that day, to assure herself, I understand now, that my body was plié-ing, tendu-ing, sashaying, tiptoeing, going. Dancing was going, an effect of my mother's grief. This is the physics of our relationship.

Did you keep dancing? my therapist asks.

I tell her yes but not in the studio. We lost our money sometime in 1990. There was a war and a flood, and together they caused an avalanche—Mama became erratic and unruly, even violent, and would disappear for a string of nights, and Papa left to salvage what he could of his business from the war. My older brother entered into a sad and angry mood that eventually led to frequent drug use. But even with the mood, my brother managed to take on the role of parent, and he found ways to make money so we could eat. There were days when we'd go without food until sundown, and the only way to ignore our hunger was to inflict pain another way. We would play with the flame of a candle, pinching it with thumb and index finger until it went out.

One way my brother made food money was to run a taxi service with the van our father left us. He was a high school junior, old enough to get a driver's license in Manila. We shuttled fellow students to and from our schools, charging them enough for a meal each way. My brother, who took piano lessons during the time I was in ballet, hadn't lost his love of music even when we had lost everything. If anything, the poverty and our family's version of orphanhood intensified his love—need—of music. The van he drove was popular among commuters because he outfitted it with cassette jackets, Super Orange car fresheners, and cases of tapes: hip-hop A-sides and B-sides. My brother was a muso—we all knew that the first day he laid fingers on a keyboard. He read notes as though he could sense them from the air; life with sound was a constant osmose for him. So he chose hip-hop, and only hip-hop, for the van and his passengers, as a way to subtract, to home in, to detract from the chaos of Manila noise, a belligerent and negligent mother, and the deafening sound of silence after one's father leaves. Hip-hop made sense to him and to me because the top tracks of the day were as angry and angsty as we were, and were cadenced lyrics from the mouths of '90s justice seekers. It felt apt. And because it felt apt, I danced to it. I popped and locked, tutted, ticked. I carried over the muscle control I developed in ballet and used it to isolate rib cage from neck and rib cage from hip, and I was as high as someone could get without the help of drugs. But my brother needed the help of drugs, even more so when Mama stole the van service from us and operated it with her lover. Without the van, without the music—what was a boy supposed to do? There was no rhythm now, not even the *grumm* of an engine, so my brother—my personal DJ—went from sad to sullen to resentfully silent. His vibrations changed. When I was in a room with him, all I could feel was the antipathy emanating from his body. And bodies communicate, so I shuffled as far away from him as I could, taking his muteness as a warning.

And you stopped dancing then? my therapist assumes. She is wrong for the first time in the months I'd been seeing her. I feel a sense of pride. Maybe I am finally the enigma she can't decode. Maybe I like to be a mystery. What child of trauma doesn't?

You'd think. But I danced in front of the mirror a lot. I had nobody, so my reflection was my company.

She writes on her clipboard and bites her lip. She is silent for a minute before she asks, *Did your reflection talk?*

My reflection didn't talk as much as she echoed. I sang a song to her and she sang it back to me. I sang a line from a song about things being gone before you knew it, first like Joni, then Janet, because at that point I was a preteen sliding on a scale of bemoaning to bewildered. Everything was equally irritating and intriguing, and add to that the fact that my brother was sent off to live with his biological father (after years of our mother keeping him away), my mother had turned into a con artist who sold nonexistent real estate, and her lover had turned the house into a breeding and fighting space for gamecocks. There were also strange men coming through the house, some of whom visited me while I slept. I woke up to memories of dreams of memories of even deeper dreams. So Joni's brooding and Janet's sultry sounds fit—ranges that both went over octaves, but one came out sounding strangulated and the other, sexed. The dance moves that I paired with their songs involved swaying, a whole lot of it, mostly with my eyes closed, at tempo with my breathing, and just briskly enough to lift the hem of my shirt or skirt into a parachute. There was joy in seeing my shirt or skirt let air come in and through the fabric. There was a soothing quality to it—that I could be touched without being touched; that something could be close but safe. Later, in college, I would see my preteen reflection in the Martha Graham dancers I watched in New York City—dancers trained in Graham's style of contraction and release, which went directly against the illusion of weightlessness given off by classical ballet. Her technique involved meaningful, cumbersome steps—the dancers leapt only to be on the ground again, gravitropic. The gold border of the hallway mirror outside my bedroom framed these steps well. It was taller than it was wide, and much of the upper portion of it served as negative space— most of the moving was done so my body would end up crouched or folded or splatted on the floor. This was laborious, and I liked it. Sweat begets sweat.

Did you ever feel separated from your reflection? Was she watching you or were you watching her?

Neither. I was watching me. I know what you're trying to get at. But I am not my mother.

My mother lived as two—at least two—people. I had described her/ them in my book and in therapy as Tiger Mama and Orchid Mama. Tiger Mama had a gun in her purse; Orchid Mama hummed while she brushed her hair or did her makeup. Mama split in two after my baby brother died, and she kept splitting, or kept going deeper into her two personalities—I lost track: Was it multiplication or division or addition?—and became scarier to us with each year. By the time I was eleven, she had habitually forgotten to feed us, had assisted her lover in multiple embezzlement scams, had flailed and shot a gun in the air, and had bathed in the rain with one breast hanging out. I had told all this to my therapist, probably by our second session, and by our fourth, she had asked permission to share an observation she'd made: *Can I tell you what I think your mother has, why she acted the way she did?* I had wanted this answer since I was three. *I think your mother is dissociated—dissociative identity disorder.*

I have read plenty about dissociative identity disorder, and I know I don't have it. I could have had it—it was right for my therapist to take note of eleven-year-old me speaking to her reflection in the mirror. But I had never been splintered. My joy was always enmeshed with my sadness, my levity with my pain. I could cry and laugh at the same time, and still do. And I have never entered amnesiac fugues. I have the opposite problem, a gift and a burden—I remember everything. Is that not why I write memoir? And is the essay not a form of uniting the multitudes within us, within me? Everything connects. I follow my body's and brain's lead.

That's not what I'm saying, my therapist says. *I know you are not your mother, and I don't think you are dissociated. I just want to know where the point was.*

What point?

When you could *have dissociated. Look, you're very strong. I really don't know how you've held up as well as you have. I am not worried about you at all. In fact, I'm fascinated by you.*

By what?

By how you've survived and thrived. You are more high functioning than most patients I have who've never been through the amount of trauma you have. I was just interested to know how you came out of all that this way, and I think I know now.

I give her the time to explain. She tells me about dance/movement therapy, the importance of paying attention to our breath, and the physicality of psychology. That muscle is memory, too—contractions and expansions of tissue that have emotional and mental provenance. That a human being is an anatomical organism, a whole made up of many smaller wholes, or systems. She asks if I kept dancing through my teen years and college, and I say yes. *Bingo,* her smile tells me. Last time she asked me to imagine my happy place, I started crying. I imagined my bed, my head on my pillow, my hands clasped in prayer. She told me to stop and open my eyes, because what I had been considering my happy place was obviously a sad place. Prayer at bedtime, she said, although sacred and important to me, might have been tinged with lonely and fearful memories. She asked me at that same session to imagine another place, and I couldn't produce one. *Let's try doing happy place again,* she says today. *Imagine yourself dancing. Four, three, two, one.*

It is my first college dance performance, and before me is an audience of two hundred. I am a spider creeping to stage left, the spotlight following me. My arms are two of eight limbs, shooting into the air like daggers, and my feet are ball-heeling in rickety syncopation; I must be frenzied. And frenzied I am. I am a black widow orbiting my mate. I luxuriate in leg movements—the tendu I had practiced since childhood, the full and demi-pliés that make me more insect than pigeon. My arm extensions are to part the web I had spooled around him, biceps and triceps and trapezius activated and in sync. *Which should I devour first, head or heart?* I say to myself, thinking back to the strangers that visited my bedside when I was asleep. The lights dim, the stage goes black. Applause.

I am scooping air out of air, my pelvis is dipping in sequential *U*s while my legs bring me forward and back. I do this, with some variation in head and hand flicks for every verse, to M.I.A.'s "Bamboo Banga." I am at the end of my college dance career; it is the last performance, in fact, and I have just decided to drop dance as a second major. I didn't want to *major* in dance, I just wanted to enjoy it. I am giving the routine all my power—or as the song says, "Powah! Powah!"—and when the techno-tribal-world track introduces the sound of dogs barking as an interjection to the chorus, my mouth opens to let out an inaudible howl, then a very loud laugh. I am standing over my prey, paws heavy on the carcass of a mammal who didn't know that my body was not their body, but mine. I am a pack leader, I belong to a tribe. I am no longer a sad, abandoned, hungry child. I just fed on the meat of someone who now knows they're weak. The song ends, I am a frozen wolf, and the class and teacher are staring with their jaws hanging.

I am a young bride of twenty-four, newly unveiled from under polyester tulle and dressed in an empire-waist sheath with a lace overlay, as light as the day's atmosphere. My groom is twirling me next to a koi pond in Central Park, while two sparrows play in a birdbath next to us. I think of us as the two sparrows, washing off trauma from our opposite but parallel pasts. My groom spins me, and my quadriceps and gluteal muscles ground my standing leg so the rest of me is ethereal, and the hem of my dress parachutes up, just like when I was little, and he keeps spinning me around until we make our exit—the hand-holding, snickering, shy little dance our recessional.

One, two, three, four. You can come back now.

I hesitate to come back but know that I have to. It is what dance has taught me to begin with: being present. I open my eyes.

Looks like you found your happy place. My therapist and I are both smiling; we have been rewarded for our work. She tells me that I should dance again, maybe find a local studio or a gym offering dance classes, and tells me that since I was diagnosed with complex PTSD, my body has likely been longing for rhythmic movement, for an excuse to be frenzied. She reminds me that I started seeing her after I had a baby, because having a baby is equal parts physical and spiritual experience. Like dance, childbirth shifts your inside and outside, and nothing is the same after. Like dance, emotions surface once dormant muscles are put to use, once your body learns it can do painful, incredible things. *It tests reality, it grounds you. You reach otherwise lost positive body memories. It reclaims your body piece by piece.*

I find a local dance studio and a gym offering cardio-dance workouts. I pay for memberships, now that I can afford them. My therapist has released me from under her care. *You have your tools now.* I feel broken up with, but also ready to move on—now that she's found me out, where's the fun? I feel like my brother when he had just been discharged from rehab, like I'm buying a new plant, unsure if I can, as the rehab counselor had instructed him, keep a plant alive. I plan on showing up for Beginner Contemporary and Beginner Hip-Hop at the dance studio, and Afro-Caribbean Cardio at the gym. I consider whether this is my new shorthand, talk therapy as once upon a time, dance as ever after.

I go every week, and I get my husband to take classes with me. It is my happy place—I can see his reflection in the studio mirror, and it is wiggling and jiggling and getting down harder than I will allow myself. He is over six feet of musculoskeletal joy reclaiming memory. Sometimes I stop in a deep squat, immobilized, my face in my hands, because the laughter is paralyzing. When we pick up our daughter from the gym day care, a woman from our class who is also picking up her child says, *Your mama and daddy like to shake it, and bless them, they bring me joy!* And we are happy to be someone else's therapy.

But then I go to a community service and prayer meeting with a bunch of old White ladies, ladies who lunch, and not only do I feel out of place in my sports tank and leggings, the "praises" I share from my week are scrutinized and compel the ladies to ask if they can lay hands on me. I say thanks but no thanks, there is no need to pray—Afro-Caribbean dance is not voodoo. They say that it is tribal, therefore pagan, and I must cancel my gym membership at once. Someone suggests I switch over to the very technical, mechanical routine of Pilates. *Pilates?!* I say, disgusted at the thought of muscle control without magic—of fixing my body without using my body to fix the rest of me. A woman says I am in dire need of prayer, for I might have summoned unwanted spirits into my life. Dance as a curse. But I don't believe her; there is nothing visible nor invisible that proves her point. My form of dance—the arm throwing, gyrating, backbending, toes reaching into pockets of air—is the visible and invisible me: reflection and person, laughter and tears, spider, wolf, woman. I get up and leave without saying goodbye, and I don't come back. I find spiritual people with leanings toward the charismatic. If dance is a summoning, it is only summoning mental health, physical strength, and deep relationships for me. I have my unlikeness to my mother to prove it. And I have a daughter watching. I see her snap and bob her head.

I become an evangelist for dance. I proselytize one woman and family after another. It is that point in the Carolina summer when even the pool isn't refreshing—the water is as warm as air in a parked car. I entice moms with an air-conditioned dance studio and a summer activity that will wear out the kids. I also text them things like And great for those experiencing depression or anxiety! Trust me! I organize an inaugural Family Hip-Hop and Creative Movement class, fifteen dollars per family. No prior experience necessary, just bring your body and your memories, and we provide the rhythm and routine. It is my mission today to make everyone crazy. Tribal crazy. Just as all of our ancestors, no matter where we hail from, used to do—gather round, pull out the lute and drum, and circle the blazing pit while flitting and frolicking. I tell everyone, *Don't be nervous. Your body just wants to tell you things.* I don't tell them we might travel in space and time, because we will come back to the present. That is the point, anyway.

Five, six, seven, eight. And—

The routine starts with two steps forward, a cross of the arms, and a nod. Step two is a whiz of the right hand to the left knee, as if we're washing a big window, and we come back to standing position by clapping our way up. From that point, there are jumps, slides across the floor, swiveling on one hand, and marking the air with punches, cutting it with leg hikes, and clutching at it as if to collect all the oxygen for later use. At water break, everyone tries to catch their breath and everyone is talking at once, but nobody is talking to one person in particular. We are all saying, *That was so hard! My legs are on fire! My arms feel like twisted noodles! I am more exhausted now than after a marathon!* But everyone is saying these things and smiling. This is painful, incredible work.

We all get back in front of the mirror, to our respective spots on the floor, sons, daughters, mothers, fathers. The music starts. One of the moms commits to her body roll, and it is the most sensual I've ever seen her. Another mom is looser than I've ever known her to be—she organizes homes and offices—and is breathing deep, breathing slow, breathing into her muscles. My daughter, who is an achiever and rule follower, is lying on the floor and doing the same moves as the rest of us but on her own lateral plane. I have succeeded, I think, because everyone is moving through time and space like their pituitary glands are regulated: thyroid is stimulated, oxytocin is high, and there's nary a trace of cortisol. The only fight-or-flight reaction here is flying en pointe to the ceiling and fighting for stability when balancing on one foot. I watched my mother dance in the rain once—she had both feet on the ground but could not maintain her balance.

I look at myself in the mirror, my reflection looking back at me. We are sweating, our clothes clinging to my/her skin, my/her sweat smells and tastes salty, like the ocean between here and there, then and now, and we are one with ourselves in this frenzy.

She is. I am.

A Triptych: The Girls
of Summer

I.

1. morena[1]
noun.

- A feminine Portuguese word meaning *tan* or *brunette* used to describe a girl with olive skin tone. A morena can be a white person with a tan and dark hair, or, more accurately, a morena can be a person of mixed race. A morena can be a person of obvious African ancestry (including someone with light or dark skin, curly, wavy or even straight hair). This word is typically used as a compliment—used like the word *babe.*

I am the mother of a six-year-old girl diving into a pool in a pink suit. The pink is a stark neon against her skin, her brown skin, the brown that the whole sun shines against. I sit reclined in a plastic pool chair, blinded by the light around me, and I shield my face with an opened book. I shield it to see her better: there are no lifeguards at the

---

1   Definition from UrbanDictionary.com; grammatical corrections mine.

neighborhood pool, so we swim at our own risk. She swims on my watch.

But I shield my face, too, as I'm learning to admit, out of habit, out of anxiety and insecurity, out of what lingers from my own childhood under the sun, or, rather, the childhood I spent guarded from it. My daughter plunges into the water, her pencil dive sending plumes of aqua into the air. I clap, the way young mothers clap at everything their young children do, even though she has done this more than a hundred times. I applaud her form and agility, her courage, her pointed toes and her arms pressed so tightly against her sides as she slips into the water like a needle. I also applaud her lack of fear of UV rays, of getting dark and getting darker. A fear I am unlearning, a fear yet to be instilled in her. I hope.

I call out, "Morena! My morena!"

Her black hair and goggles tilt out of the water.

"Snack time, morena!" I say, pulling out a Tupperware of chips from the beach bag. I wave the container in the air, enticing her with it. "Come, have a snack! You can get back in the water, I promise!"

She wades to the steps and walks to me, her pink and brown coming into clearer view. I wrap her in a towel so that the towel hangs from her bony shoulders, but it falls off as soon as she reaches forward for her snack. Her arm extended, I grab it so she can't get away, and I fumble for the spray can of sunscreen in my bag. I uncap it as she protests, "You said it was snack time!"

"It is, it is. I just want to reapply some before you get back in again," I say as I spray her.

"Yeah, but now I have to wait for it to dry," she says, wiggling her arm out of my grip as a fog of zinc oxide chases after her skin.

"You can eat while it dries." I kiss her pout into a smile. "I brought cookies, too."

She fits herself next to me on the plastic chair and her one side rubs against my sundress as she reclines. I think, *Oh, great. Now it's rubbed off.* I consider spraying her again, but I don't want to be pushy. I don't want to be pushy because I don't want to be like my parents, who detested the sun, and who detested that I did not detest the sun. My daughter pencil dives and nosedives and springboards into water—she knows no other prelude or epilogue to these jumps than my cheering and clapping. But again, I consider respraying. I think about it for a second—*Will she really look like a farmer?*—then I see from over my shoulder that her arms and chest are the electric purplish-white color of zinc, particularly zinc on brown skin, zinc that is seeping into epidermis to form a light-deflecting barrier. I am relieved. I may not prohibit outdoor living, but I feel better knowing that my spray can aim was accurate, and that I, the mother, have done something to avoid what the doctors and mom-bloggers say to avoid: sun poisoning, burning, blistering, cancer. I am a good mom for this. But am I? What about the lies I may or may not still believe? Believing is automatic thinking. It is perception uninterrupted, unremitted, uncontested. At least I stop and think about how this could be wrong: that the darker you are, the lower you sit on the Philippine socioeconomic ladder.

"Mama, can you buy a different kind next time? I look purple," she says, putting the lid on the now empty Tupperware. She licks powdered cheese off her fingers and wipes both hands on her towel, then works to rub the sunscreen in. She is worried about looking purple, and I think, *At least she's not worried about looking dark or black.*

I help buff the zinc in until it's near-invisible, and I say, "We'll get a different kind when this runs out, my Mim-mim." Mim-mim is the name of the giant purple bunny she watches on TV.

"Or we can just not use any, Mom. So much time putting on sunscreen!" She holds her arms out in a T to show me just how much time we spend on the routine. "More swim time, more!"

"I guess it's okay to go without it sometimes," I say, shrugging, but remind her that we are at the pool every day, that we do get plenty of swim time. But I do not remind my family that. The last time they visited, which was two summers ago, I got lectured for how little time I spent cooking and how much time we spent outdoors. My papa was staying with us in South Carolina after his stroke so he could take a break from long walks to the subway and from the stress of the city, and so I could encourage him to do water aerobics—a suggestion from his physical therapist. He stayed with us for three weeks and put on his swim shorts once, but he never got in the water, and never stepped outside for longer than a six-minute walk with the dog down to the street corner and back.

"The sun in South Carolina is like the sun in the Philippines," he said. "It bakes you."

"It won't kill you," I said. "And how's it any different from the sun in Saudi?"

My father lived in Saudi Arabia from 1979 through 1985, and frequently traveled there on business until the mid-'90s. "Pero people there don't just lie out in the sun like Americans do."

"We are not *just* lying in the sun. We are trying to get you to walk and move normally," I said, gathering the pool noodle for him and the floatie for my girl.

"I can exercise in your apartment," he said, sitting back down on the sofa and reaching for the remote.

"But you don't. You just sit here and watch."

"Mama, let's go!" my daughter pleaded as she sweated under her rash guard.

"Fine," I said as I turned toward the door. "Pa, we'll try tomorrow, okay? We're there almost every day."

He turned on the television without replying, so we walked to the door with all our pool toys, snacks, and of course, the zippered bag of sunscreen bottles, and as we were about to step out, my father said, "Every day, I know. That's why your daughter is negra now. Your sister agrees."

I didn't say anything, just like I had never said anything, not in response to the negra comment, or to the comments about looking like a dark farmer, an uneducated and uncivilized tribeswoman, or a low-class Indio that other family members and family friends had previously made about my appearance. I checked to see if my daughter heard what Papa said, and she was pretending to blast fireballs at a spider web hanging from the ceiling—engaged in imaginary play and oblivious to, I liked to believe, the fireball just thrown at me, *and her*, by my father. This was the same father that scooped more ice cream into my bowl than his, who taught me how to draw Superman, and who put me up on his shoulders, pointed to the night sky, and showed me Orion and Cassiopeia. He was the same father who quoted Jesus, Paul, and the Pope, and who prayed with me at bedtime and told me to love my neighbor as myself. He wasn't, however, the person who taught me to love myself *as* myself—there is no such person in our family, nor in our culture.

"See you later, Pa. Text me if you need anything." I shut the door behind me.

II.

2. morena[2]
   Sp. adjective.
   Tagalog
   • brown color, brown-skinned (morena/moreno: feminine/masculine) [syn. kayumanggi (brown), kulay-kape (coffee-colored), kastanyo (roasted chestnut)]

Today I am less milky tea and more coconut husk, but not quite strong coffee or pure cacao—I am not quite *there* yet. But I am well on my way, if I keep playing soccer, my brother's wife reminds me. We have been

---

2   Definition from Tagalog-Dictionary.com

sitting in this car for almost two hours, stuck in the usual Manila traffic, and this is what we talk about when we run out of snacks and there's barely any car movement. Our driver pulls his lower lip over his top teeth and shakes his head at the gridlock before us, but he does not comment, because this is what we pay him to do: drive and listen to us talk or bicker. We have not moved in twenty minutes; the rosary on the rearview mirror hangs still. It is as still as the eyes I don't dart back at my brother's wife as she talks—brags—about the wonders and benefits of papaya soap. She says because of it, she is the soft color of seashell, but to me she is the yellow brown of hemp rope that has been soaking in salt water at the edge of the pier. She goes on about how papaya proteinase lifts off dead skin cells and dark, scarred layers of the skin, and I tune her out because I am a teenager. And I tune her out because I just want to play soccer and I don't want to be bothered with looking like food, or drink, or the wood on someone's floor or side paneling. I start daydreaming about the tricks I want to do on the field: Could I do a Beckham and bend it? Could I score record goals like Hamm? Maybe flip backward like Pelé?

"Look, you are so close to tsokolate!" my brother's wife says as she interrupts my fantasizing. She grabs my arm and brings it to her face, and I can feel her breath on my skin. "Tsk." She clicks her tongue in disapproval. It is the click of the tongue that I've heard from superiors at school when I've been too talkative, and the click of the tongue that takes me back to the time when my mother held up my arm to her arm, side by side, to compare how much Spanish blood filtered into her and how little into me. She said that day that I had the coloring of a maid and not of a doctor and businessman's daughter. *Tsk!*

"Tsk!" My sister-in-law clicks her tongue again. And because I am a teenager, I yank my arm back to my side of the back seat with a young athlete's strength, so that we both recoil and hit our elbows against each of our car doors. I pretend my elbow doesn't hurt and turn to look out the window, and there, there, of course, is a nonescape from the topic at hand: billboards for skin-whitening products—roll-on, lather on, laser. I just want to get to the soccer field, run out, pull my socks over my shin guards, and kick a damn ball.

Finally, the car moves. We inch and inch and inch, then the driver slams on the accelerator and we are on the flyover that deposits our ride to the edge of the city: green grass, white lines, kids in cleats. I grab my knapsack and water and exit the car. Before I slam the door, my brother's wife ducks her head to see me and sneer at my dark brownness a final time, and says, "Hoy, sunscreen! You don't want to end up an uncivilized Ita!"

III.

3. morena[3]

noun.

Spanish

- Derived from the Moors, who ruled Spain for 800 years, who are of Arab extraction. Therefore, a person of darker complexion than the lighter European races that have inhabited Spain.
- This derivation has been largely forgotten and now refers to any woman of dark complexion (most likely in former Spanish colonies).

Eight years into marriage, in the days of overtime and meal plans and babysitters, my husband emails me an article from the website of the *Atlantic*. This is part of how we love each other now. I am on deadline for the final pass on my first book and he is teaching a full-time load plus tutoring hours, and our daughter has just entered the world of school and after-school activities. While we love to talk at dinnertime and reserve a couple nights a week for watching TV together, it is through the articles, essays, memes, GIFs, poems of the day, and Spotify

---

3   Definition from UrbanDictionary.com; grammatical corrections mine.

playlists that we email to each other that we most consistently give and receive love. Today the circle on the corner of my Gmail app icon is red, and I click on it to see whether, in this instance, red is the color of stress (from: work) or the color of romance (from: husband).

The title reads: "The Desirability of Storytellers | Among Filipino hunter-gatherers, storytelling is valued more than any other skill, and the best storytellers have the most children." I do not click on the link, baffled by why my husband would send me an article about Filipinos who have the most children. We both repeatedly and adamantly express a desire to remain as a family of three. I am not having more babies. The phrase *hunter-gatherers* also throws me off—I am not a hunter-gatherer. I think, *Well, great, the White man I married was ignorant after all.* I am not a hunter-gatherer, I am not *of* hunter-gatherers, and I would never want to be one. I am educated, from the city—the *capital*—and I have Spanish blood in me. Both of my parents assured me of this growing up. In my head, I start to sound like my mother, my father, and every other postcolonial Filipino I know: I am not tribal, I am not indigenous. I know my Catholic saints and my "Ave Maria." I am not Ita.

I don't click on the link and I don't mention it at dinner. But he asks, and I tell him I didn't have the time—two Skype calls on top of edits today. Our lines are usually open, online and in person, but tonight I choose to lie about why I hadn't read the article. I am so offended by *hunter-gatherer* and irked by the thought of having more children that I lie to him. I have only lied to him maybe four times in eight years, and all four times it was me covering up the fact that I had lost my keys or glasses again. *They were just here, I swear. I put them in my bag, I promise.* But tonight was a true lie, the lie of all lies, and I'd rather sin this way than admit to him that I felt insulted by an article he sent. I lie to not open up dialogue. I lie because I cannot admit to him why I really did not click on the link: I can hear my so-called antiracist, activist self (who once spoke about resistance, neocolonialism, and fake news in a PEN America interview) think colorist, classist postcolonial thoughts. I do not open up dialogue so that I don't have to admit to my own hypocrisy. I do not tell him that instead I started a new decoy email folder labeled "Research" and saved his email in it, in case I could pull it out as a *take that!* card in a later, more deserving argument, when, perhaps, I am lecturing him on movie night or at dinner about *his* ignorance, privilege, and hypocrisy.

Six months roll by, the book is out in the world, and it is summertime. We have exchanged countless emails since, mostly screenshots of reviews of the book—mostly good and heart-warming, some bad and worth laughing together about. We have also both downloaded the Bitmoji app—an app that allows you to create an avatar of yourself: your moods, your outfits, your physical attributes. The Bitmoji moods are easy to match with my #currentmood, and the outfits are a joy to put together. It is in the making of *me*, the physical me, that I stumble. Hair is easy: an angled bob of black hair. The body type, sure: petite but no muscle. But facial features: oof. I scroll one way and I look European, I scroll the other way and I look Malaysian, Bengali, North African, West African. But I want to look Filipino, even though I'm not sure what Filipino looks like. Is my avatar supposed to look like what I really look like, or what I am told I should look like? Is what I really look like not what I really look like—did I really damage my skin, my appearance, by spending too much time in the sun? By playing soccer, did I create a mantle over what my ancestors have passed on to me? Who are my ancestors anyway? Spanish, my parents would say. But how do you explain my nose, my lips, my color—*coloring*?

I settle for a small, round nose, which I have, and full, mauve lips, which I also have, and then I color in myself: the rosier of the two taupes I've narrowed my choices down to. But I second-guess my design—my digital imprint of self-perception—and scroll just a bit farther to the right to a tawny shade. It looks accurate in that it doesn't look yellow or green—that's for other Southeast Asian people, according to my high school social studies teacher. It is, as I only know how to put it, less milky tea and more coconut husk, but not quite strong coffee or pure cacao.

The avatar is finished; I am now a Bitmoji. I send one of "me" eating a taco to my husband. It is so large and cute on the screen that I have to send another one: "me" holding a soccer ball and watching the World Cup on TV. She/I is/am so lovable on the screen, I send Bitmoji texts to friends in New York, Los Angeles, Miami, and Frankfurt.

But then there is work. There is always work: a book tour and essays and a new collection and a class I'm teaching in the fall. I search my mind, my shoeboxes of index cards and photos, and my email inbox for fodder. The personal is political: is this not the mantra for my work—creative nonfiction? There is a folder named "Research" on the sidebar of my Gmail dashboard, and I don't know what it is. I open it and there is one, just one, item: the Filipino hunter-gatherers article. *Oh right*, I think, *personal is political*. And this one felt really personal when my husband sent it to me. I open it and there is the link, still black rather than the clicked-on blue, and I hover my arrow in a back-and-forth dance before I finally hit it, open a new tab, and read. I read and read. The article sings high praise for a Philippine indigenous group, the Agta, or Aeta, tribe in particular. I think, *Pfft*, at first, because the journalist is looking through a White lens and maybe that is why he is so fascinated with my people—*those people*— yet another man from across the ocean discovering a Brown species. But I look at the byline and there is his Asian last name, Yong. *I'll keep reading*, I decide. I scroll down and back up to reread the findings and anecdotes arranged into this "popular science" essay. I am learning new things about the Aeta people, including the fact that they value their storytellers more than they do their hunters, foragers, and fishers. The article highlights the Aeta's understanding of storytelling's adaptive value, meaning that it contributes to human evolution and to the building of an operating society. It says, "In fact, the Agta seemed to value storytelling *above all else*." The Aeta see storytellers as creative types who have a suite of attractive personality traits, making them "more attractive sexual partners." This tribe's chroniclers have 0.5 more children than the average tribesman, signaling that there is economic value to their occupation—more kids may mean more resources, or that there is allotment afforded them by their role. They are also seen as repositories of knowledge. They explain how and why things are—they pass down stories, which means they pass down identity. They are the tribe's nucleus.

The findings show that the better the storytellers are within the community, the more likely it is for them to foster equitable practices. When tribesmen share stories, they promote cooperation, egalitarianism, and gender equality. Female hunters within the Aeta tribe hunt as much as the men do, and their hunting success rate, as I find out through a quick online search, is at 31 percent. Aeta men have a success rate of only 17 percent, and they have to ask the women to help them. Is this not, in our modern terms, girl power?

So why, in my thirty-two years across two continents, have I been told by my kin, my supposed tribe, to not end up an Ita? The word *Ita*, beyond (beneath!) what it means to the culture of my sun-fearing family, is a transposition of some letters from the words *Aeta* and *Negrita*, the latter a diminutive of Negra. Black. When Miguel López de Legazpi docked his ship in our islands in the name of the viceroyalty of Spain in 1564, it was the iron-weapon-wielding highlander people of the Aeta tribe that he referred to as Negritos, or the blacks of the Pacific. And it is this fear of black skin, black culture, black sophistication and intellect that he passed down to governor after governor, and from governor to governed. My family is Catholic: we love our neighbors as ourselves. But we do not love ourselves. We fear the enemy, and, as we've been taught by López de Legazpi and the men and women that came by the shipful after him, the enemy is us. The enemy is me.

This is one way my husband and I love each other: we email. I reply to the original message he sent six months back and admit to not having read it until now. I write that we should go to the pool after we're done with work, and that we can talk about the article then. We go to the pool in the afternoon, we sit in the sun, and I start with, "Who knew that the Aeta have such girl power?" I tell him about all else I've found on the internet, and about how my perception of a people has changed because of the article he sent, and I say, "Thank you." Six months ago, I felt insulted by a gesture that was meant to say he was interested in everything and anything that might have to do with me. I took it then as a slight on who I was and what I looked like, and today I am sharing with him about childhood, soccer, Manila traffic, the Spaniards, the Aeta. He reaches into the cooler for an ice-cold LaCroix without breaking eye contact with me, a presmile on his face, and I feel valued for what I contribute to our family—stories. Again I say, "Thank you," because this article he sent me has not only changed my perception of a people, it has changed my perception of *me*.

Our daughter is in a rash guard, and I don't bother to spray her with sunscreen. My husband is still looking and presmiling at me, so coy and comfortable and married, and I am looking and smiling at our daughter. Her toes curl over the edge of the pool, her arms are pressed into her sides. She bends at the knees to build force, and with all her power, rockets off and breaks the water's surface: brown breaking blue. Her flesh slaps against $H2O$ molecules and parts them. She is solid matter. And inside her are more molecules: DNA, data, memory. The dominance of color is something I have passed down to her, but it is the moments I remember, the ones I tell and retell—to her and to myself—that we make into our only inheritance. Our birthright: to be brave and to be true.

Genealogy

This is Purefield County of the upper Piedmont region of South Carolina. The hills roll here, like the way it sounds when the people talk. Words roll off their tongues like hay bales unspooling onto the field, unhurriedly yet easily, with intention but without labor, every syllable pregnant with pride and history and story. Every field in Purefield County is fertile, every square mile home to the creatures of a pond or the pines or a pasture. The first settler to come to the area was Thomas Nightingale. His love of horses and cows drew him here in 1740, and by *here* I mean the wide fields between the Broad and the Wateree Rivers, the fair meadows bursting with wild Queen Anne's lace—the pure fields. Nightingale and other settlers stopped here in the mid-eighteenth century, grateful for a place to rest on their journey west. But the settlers never left; they tilled the soil, brought cotton to plant, and cotton they planted and harvested until the boll weevil killed the crops in the 1920s and they switched to farming cows, then turkeys. They also planted and harvested the seeds of the Bible, hopefully on good soil as the book teaches, and reaped what they sowed, fruit of every variety: Baptist, Methodist, Universalist, Presbyterian.

Between the houses here are barns for turkeys and cattle, and many silos sit between the barns, tall and short, narrow and wide. The soil here rests atop granite, on which many have relied for their livelihood. Purefield has been supplying the world with the "silk of the trade" for buildings and monuments for as long as it has been difficult, then costly, then unlawful to supply it with cotton picked by a slave. When it is not supplying the world with rock, fiber, poultry, veal, or milk, Purefield County, which used to be ancient Cherokee and Catawba territory, provides a sportsman's playground—a place to bait and hook and shoot and kill.

You can do anything in these pastures, between the silos and barns, and nobody will catch you. The only things that might are the clotheslines strung between backhouses and back porches. If you're from here, or you've come to know here like I have, you know to stay away from these clotheslines, for where a clothesline is, there a Purefield County woman of strong conviction is also. These are the women who rule the town from their rocking chairs or porch swings, and while rocking or swinging, allocate farm budgets, hire and fire hands, dictate which crop or kind of animal to farm next. These are the women who pray for their grandbabies and great-grandbabies at night—after they pray for their enemies. And their enemies are the newcomers and Yankees and metropolitan folk who want change, who try and fail to bring it. The women that hung these clotheslines and hang clothes on them in the morning and retrieve the clothes in the afternoon, also know—*decided*—where the rifles and pistols hang in the house, which room, which wall, for whose hand they have to be within reach. But yes, you can do anything in these pastures, so long as you don't get caught by the clotheslines. So long as you don't get caught by the women who hung them.

———

Genealogy: The first Clarson of the line from whom my husband hails was Richard, who settled on the south side of the Appomattox, where it joined the James, in 1652.

His descendant, Richard Jr., settled in Halifax County, North Carolina, in 1756.

His son, Richard III, moved to what is now the Fayetteville Community, Purefield County, in 1775.

David R. Clarson, the patriarch of the Clarson family in Purefield, was born in Halifax County, North Carolina, May 19, 1765. His son, born to his wife, Esther Roe, was named Drake Roe. Drake Roe lived and died on the land first settled by his father, and this land is still in the possession of their descendants, who, in letters and newspapers archived in the Purefield County History Museum, have been referred to as "numbered among the best citizens." Drake Roe named his son Dylan Alexander, who farmed the land his father bequeathed.

In this line there has been a Jacob, son of John, who married Isabelle Clarson, daughter of David P. Clarson, the best man, his descendants believe, who ever lived. There, too, was a J. Fayette Clarson Cameron, who was a man of education and refinement, described in the family's genealogy books as "a nobleman of the day." Generations later, many sons will defend the Confederacy, fight against the Yankees, and resist Union soldiers ransacking and collecting items from their homes and fields. A few of their women will opt to be harassed by a Northerner rather than surrender the house or the family hound, and some will pull the rifle's trigger to protect the farm, the harvest, the baby. Several will become fox hunters, hatmakers, home doctors. A few of their brothers and beloveds will join the Klan. One obituary reads: *He was as game as a Ku Klux to the day of his death, which occurred in May 1873.*

The Clarsons documented much of their lives on these upcountry pastures, in what would become hardbound genealogy books; a book of maps; diaries; ledgers; and a sketchbook of antebellum architecture. In several of these books, it is noted that the Clarsons of the eighteenth and nineteenth centuries were "long-lived and splendid types of physical manhood, the average weight about 220 lbs., and most of the Clarsons over six feet tall."

My husband is over six feet tall. But he weighs far less than the rest of them—his leanness I attribute to basketball, but also to his lack of interest in the family trade of farming and the family hobby of hunting. We met in New York City, where his high school teachers predicted he would end up after adolescence, and where he explored—escaped to—the world of the arts and languages, of Korean and Cuban food, concerts, off-Broadway shows, galleries and museums, and the bars and boutiques in SoHo. He is very different from the Clarson fox hunters, turkey and cow farmers, and land- and slave-owning homesteaders of historical times. Unlike two of his cousins who attended the Citadel, South Carolina's military college, and his father and grandfather who served in the military, my husband has no interest in combat. He would much rather paint watercolors, learn a second and a third language, or play a thrifted vinyl on the record player.

But he is kind and quiet like the rest of them. For this they can pardon his eccentricities. It was just too bad that during his time in New York City (as his grandmama has said, *of all places—God bless his soul*), he met a girl and eventually married her. The girl, of course, is me, and I am Filipino, the dark-skinned, formerly undocumented kind, too. And this is the fact that changes it all, for of all the Clarsons of the Carolina upcountry, he is the first to marry a person of color.

———

I walked through the door only twenty minutes ago and Grandmama— my husband's maternal grandmother—has already told me all the town's news from the month: that the Clarson bachelor didn't invite her to his wedding this Saturday, that my husband's first cousins went on holiday for their anniversary, that the Mrs. three doors down took her grandson (whom she never sees) to the ball game, that some other Mrs. remarried, that a boy came home and bought a trailer so he could live close to his mama. I should not forget that she mentioned which of the cousins purchased new farm equipment—new equipment means change: new crop, new animals to breed and sell, new ways of doing things. She tells me again, *I don't know why I wasn't invited to the weddin'.* I tell her I packed a dress—I'd take her to crash the wedding. *That's sweet,* she says, *but I'm not much for going to things anymore. I don't mean I want to go. I just don't know why I couldn't.* And I know she means this; she's not trying to be nice. Perhaps of all her traits, it is her directness I most admire. Grandmama and I agree very little on how to live, what makes a good life, what makes a good person, but I like that she never dillydallies and she says what she means. She's a talker, and she talks only about what she thinks is true. She tells me all the facts, all of Purefield County's truths, the details of the past and the present. Good fodder for narrative, I often think.

Today she tells me the truth about her health, or what she thinks about her health. She's been going blind since my baby, who is now six, was born. She used to sew but now can't tell a strand of hair from a piece of cotton thread. We don't move things around her house when we come over from Charleston, about two and a half hours away. We don't move things because she knows where they are from memory. Her macular degeneration, a hereditary condition that clouds all but peripheral vision, is exacerbated by her weak knees and hypertension. Can't see, can't stand too long, can't think too much, can't feel too strongly. She might as well be the wild flowers picked from the field, that sit in a vase on the kitchen table until they are no longer bright and perky.

I'm gathering that she feels as though her world is shrinking, vanishing. She can't even read her newspaper all too well anymore. She can't keep up with the goings-on of the world. She can't dial the phone now either—the numbers are too small to see. So Grandmama has to wait for her last living child and her nine grandchildren and twenty great-grandchildren to call. When they do call, the conversations are short and pithy, but enough. She tells me she uses a magnifying glass to read the cards and letters she receives from them in the mail, and she tells me how long it takes to get from *Dear* to *PS.* It takes all day to do anything now, all day to wring the wash, walk to the clothesline, hang the clothes up, and get back in before the sun burns her neck as it bleaches the linens. *I try to walk to the clothesline. That's my exercise. But, Lord, take me if I ever have a stroke. I have no patience to wait, no patience to recover. May the Lord take me then.*

I have no living grandparents of my own, so the thought of her having a stroke is saddening. I never thought I'd be so affected by her sentiments and ailments, especially since she was originally adamantly opposed to my having married S—her last living daughter's only son. She is next to the stove and crying now, saying, *I prayed every night that God would give me healthy grandchildren and great-grandchildren. It's not easy not being well.*

I feel like crying, too, but I remember that she can't think too much, can't feel too strongly, so I stop myself and make a diversion. I tell her that I sold another book to a publisher, an essay collection, only a couple of months after the release of my first one. I fascinate her with names of cities I've visited on my book tour, the number and kinds of people I've met, the types of questions reporters asked me at interviews, the museum exhibits I visited last time I was in New York, and the topics I hope to write about next. Even though she can't see, she doesn't break eye contact with me, and she says, *Well, thank the Lord,* at the end of every one of my stories. My news is her news now. Her world may be shrinking, vanishing, but with me are tales I've brought from beyond the Broad and the Wateree Rivers, from upriver, up north, and down home in the Lowcountry. I siphon into her quiet and blurring world specifics from the world out there—names, dates, and events, details of man's passing in time.

———

When my husband's family talks about heritage, they talk about land. They talk about where the quarries are, where the pines are being logged, where the cows graze, where the hounds find the dead or injured fox.

But of course they are also talking about who let all that happen, who said, *Okay, give it a go,* to the granite diggers, the loggers, the dairy farmers, and the hunters who go back into town after a weekend of outdoor leisure in a rented portion of the country.

Now, what they don't talk about is who gave permission to the Clarsons and good ol' Thomas Nightingale to settle here. Whosoever said, *Okay, give it a go,* to the men who came in horse-drawn buggies, pitched tents, drafted boundaries, and later on built cabins, a church, an academy. The thing is, nobody said those words. Certainly not the Cherokee and Catawba people that governed civilizations between the Broad and Wateree, who fished in these parallel rivers, and who ate the small game caught in these woods—these words do not appear in the history and genealogy books.

But I will give it to one of the authors of *Purefield County South Carolina: A Pictorial History,* published in 1989, the admittance of two things: First, that he often stumbled upon handmade bricks, doll heads, fort ruins, and seven-thousand-year-old Native American points, or arrowheads, during his twenty-two years as a forester in the area—proving that there was thriving life here before the settlers came; and second, that African Americans had played and continued to play important roles in Purefield County, but their contributions were not adequately represented in the photographs made available to him and his coauthor. Yet he summarizes the history of Purefield County as a sort of coexistence: the greenspace between the rivers where Catawba met Cherokee, and where the upcountry indigo, cattle, and silk farmer met the Lowcountry rice planter and his slaves. Like a party upriver, sans the bunting and cake, where everyone eventually, casually, agreed that the in-between of the Broad and the Wateree Rivers was now under the jurisdiction of a small group of Scotch-Irish clans.

But let's go back to who said what.

In 2011, cousin A joined the world of online dating. She was the last singleton of the nine Clarson grandchildren. Everyone prayed she would find "the one." When she spoke of having gone on a few dates with a Haitian man and of plans to bring him to Grandmama's on Thanksgiving, the other grandchildren said, *Hell, no! Grandmama would not appreciate that.*

I remember asking why it would be such a bad idea.

And they said it just was, it goes against peacekeeping in the family.

I said, *You all gave me such a hard time when I started dating S—and I'm not even Black. I don't want to know what you guys would've said or done had I been Black.*

That was different, they said. *You're different. We love you, don't forget that. We love you. Grandmama loves you, that's all that matters.*

———

I first visit Purefield County in the summer of 2009, to meet S's dying aunt, Julia, and to receive Grandmama's blessing. I have been dating S since the winter of 2006, but nothing has necessitated a visit to his maternal hometown until now. We have started talking about marriage—he envisions a wedding where our families would share space and air and merriment, while I simply, selfishly, want to elope. He's always been the optimist in our relationship, and I the cynic coming out of years of trauma. However the legal union is going to play out, there is no question that we need Grandmama's blessing, and we can only avoid her for so long. I have left my family in New York—this is family now. And should something happen to either me or S, like illness or unemployment or an accident, these are now the people we can look to. But that connection, that *relationship*, requires a formality—a sort of rite of passage that I can only guess is part of being Scotch-Irish, with the idea of clans, but also part of the makeup of Purefield itself: for generations, the Clarsons only married offspring from the Feastons, Millers, and Bulls—Purefieldians dating back to the 1700s and whose lineage can also be traced to the same Richard and Esther. Whoever dared to stray from this pattern married and left for Alabama, Mississippi, or Pennsylvania, or went out West where they spoke of gold.

S's aunt Julia has battled cancer twice and has chosen to live her last days outside of treatment. Although it is our first meeting, I have previously felt her warmth through what was said of her, or what was said of what she has said in defense of me. One story relayed to me: In the thick of therapy and hair loss, she sat through a baby shower in the basement of her mother's church, telling Grandmama that just because I was from New York, it didn't mean that I was a damn Yankee, and that just because I was Brown, it didn't mean that I committed crimes that Brown people supposedly did. Grandmama had apparently pulled out a newspaper clipping during the baby shower, a news article about a Latina who had committed a felony, and said, waving the clipping in the air, *See, Margaret? See?* Margaret is S's mother, who has also done her fair share of defending me.

The first time I walk into Grandmama's house, I am waif thin from being college broke and wearing Bermuda-length jean shorts I cut from a pair of pants, a pinstriped Chloé tuxedo shirt, and camel-colored heels that can translate from day to night. My entire wardrobe is this way, a collection of takeaways from a Garment District job, my fashion-school friends' projects, and thrifts from New York's ubiquitous flea markets. I want to dress for the occasion or the location—a farm, in this case—but today my style looks, accidentally, Olsen-twin-chic. So, I am conscious of my appearance during our two-hour ride, and I have never been conscious, in the shy or apprehensive way, of my appearance before. I feel like I have tried to quiet my look but can't, so instead I resolve to quiet myself. The plan is to stay as silent as possible today, to counter the loudness, yet me-ness, of my outfit, but also to refrain from starting what could become an argument.

S enters the house first, because I make him, and I trail behind like a coy child hiding under her mother's skirt. *What are you doing?* he says. *This is weird.*

Well, so is everything else. I feel like Marie Antoinette about to meet the French, I say, jokingly, but also to hurt his feelings just a bit, because he has, after all, been born to a family yet to meet a Brown future in-law.

In response, in retaliation really, he curls his arm back and around me, swivels me to where everyone can see me, and says, *Well, here she is.*

I wave. They all sit in a semicircle in the den, some in rocking chairs, some on the sofa, the rest on pillows on the floor. I don't count how many of them are here, but I take note of how many more people there are than chairs. They sit in the semicircle as if waiting for the theater curtains to part and the show to begin, and all I can do is wave and say hello.

Grandmama, this is Cinelle, S says, smiling.

She stares briefly and then says hello. Nobody else says much after introducing themselves. S pulls his lower lip up over his teeth, thinking of what to say next, swallowing his spit, thinking more. My hand is still in the air, but my wave is now a slow flutter, the wings of a dying dragonfly. *Say something, dammit.* I bend over to give Grandmama our first hug. She doesn't hug me back as much as she folds her arm to pat my back, twice and no more.

At last, Aunt Julia says, *Well, lady, I have been* dying *to meet you.* I get the joke and laugh, but everybody else thinks it's morbid—eyes big and unblinking. This is when I know that she is an ally, and that if I sit next to her the entire day, I'll be fine. She pats the small space next to her on the sofa, and I walk over toward her, sit, and nod as she points out each relative and says a little about each one. I grin every time S looks back to mouth, *You okay?*

We sit until we are called to the dinner table, where Margaret has set a spread of green bean casserole, pineapple casserole, chicken casserole, and rolls. Today I learn that the Clarsons, like most farming families, call lunch *dinner* and call dinner *supper.* Because farmers wake and work before sunrise, by noon, they are ready for their dinner.

No one speaks during the meal, not even Aunt Julia, who labors to consume the contents of her plate. I keep with her pace. It is the slowest I have ever chewed my food, the first time I might actually know what it means to masticate. The silence is very unlike my Filipino family. We are always eating while talking, talking while eating, talking about the next meal while consuming the meal in front of us, and planning tomorrow's grocery list and the route we will take to make it to all our favorite markets: the Asian market, the Filipino store, and Western Beef.

When Margaret serves derby pecan pie, people shuffle to different parts of the house with slices of it in hand, the clinking of dessert spoons on dessert plates the only sounds filling the moth-ball-scented rooms. Aunt Julia has grown tired and wants to take a nap, and I think, *Oh no,* afraid of her absence. Even S is a silent creature in the house. I have always taken him for an introvert, but the kind who breaks dance floors at weddings and the kind that I dated long-distance for three years, our relationship relying on three-hour phone calls. This uncommunicativeness is what I consider as his first betrayal of me: his morphing into a foreign and nimble creature whenever family is nearby. But I can't get mad at him at the moment; I have to keep my cool. I look for ways to pass time. I walk through the house, which is longer than it is wide, with rooms stemming from one main hall, the walls of which are covered with portraits of children, grandchildren, great-grandchildren, and ancestors, all in their Sunday best. A bed sits in the middle of each room, the sheets starched from the sunlight pouring in through wall-to-wall windows. In each room, too, stands a dresser or built-in shelf filled with hardbounds: photo albums, Bibles, books.

I softly say, *Excuse me,* as I enter each room, walk past a relative eating pie, and ease toward a section of the family archive. I have always been one to talk in congenial settings, but since the farmhouse seems to be inhabited only by murmurs and whispers and Grandmama's litanies overheard from a distance, I busy myself with the curation on the dressers and shelves. I feel each leather spine, palm over each title, and thumb the pages' edges. I only flip through the ones that have pages that are more white than yellow, the less ancient-looking ones, and read only the first page or two, afraid that something might rip or fall out. I look most thoroughly through the albums, which are extensions of the stories told through the photos on the wall: generations of cow herding and dairy farming, Kmart shopping and portrait studios, Sunday school and baptisms, weddings held at the local church and on the farm.

When I make it back to the den, where Grandmama has kept the majority of the books, two hours have passed and some people have fallen asleep on the sofa and in rocking chairs. S looks exhausted from keeping Grandmama company and keeping her, I understand now, away from me. He has said *Yes, ma'am* about a thousand times, appeasing her by agreeing with everything she has to say: about the weather, about politics, about the Psalms, and about this thing she has only started hearing about—Facebook.

In midreach for a spine that says *The Genealogy of Purefield County*, I hear my name.

Cinelle, come on over here. Grandmama sits where Aunt Julia was when we first arrived, and she pats the space next to her to beckon me over. *Those books are very special to the family. I reckon you like to read?*

I like books, ma'am. I have subconsciously adopted the family's vernacular—I have never referred to anyone as *ma'am* before.

S tells me you're a writer. We've never had a real writer in the family, I mean someone who publishes.

Yes, ma'am.

We got plenty of books about our folks. Now tell me about your folks.

I tell her my mother is a physician, my father a businessman, and two of my siblings live in New York. I don't say that my mother is mentally ill and has lost her medical license, or that my father left when I was eight, or that I have lost a baby brother to prematurity and almost lost another one to drug overdose. I don't say I was adopted

120

as a teenager. And I don't talk about being undocumented, since she already knows and has fixated on this fact for three years. I mention having fifty-two aunts, uncles, cousins, nieces, and nephews in New York, thinking that perhaps she'd appreciate that my kin, like her kin, stay close to each other. I share a few pleasantries: how nice to have books for heirlooms, how tasty the pie was, how I should have worn flats instead of heels so as not to pill her carpet. I am now uncorked and I keep talking, continually but still cautiously, and before I know it, the sun is coming down, the cousins are leaving, and it is time for us to go. Grandmama has sat with me, listening for over an hour and saying *I reckon* and *I declare,* adjusting her hearing aids when she can't make out what I am saying.

I appreciate you talkin', she says, patting me on the back, eyes welling up with tears as we say our goodbyes, looking at me with hollow eyes, as if to beg for more, as if she's been hungry, for God knows how long, for someone to finally speak.

———

It is the summer of 2015. We visit Grandmama at the beginning of June, on our way back to Charleston after my MFA graduation. She is going to attend my graduation party later in the week, but we think that paying her a visit at her home in Purefield County is a nice gesture—she has helped put me through grad school by sending twenty- and fifty-dollar bills in the mail or slipping them in my purse at Thanksgiving. I have brought with me a haul of books, folders, and my first full manuscript—what will become my debut book, *Monsoon Mansion*—in a large blue polypropylene bag from IKEA. This is the only bag I own of this size, and the only container I have that can hold all the literature I consumed and produced during my two years practicing the craft of creative nonfiction. I want to sort and rearrange its contents while at Grandmama's house, because the unpaginated and unstapled pages have shuffled around the trunk during our drive and kept waking up our toddler, who was sleeping in the car seat. So while we won't be staying long at her place, I take the blue bag out of the car and place it in her den, with the intention of sorting through it once Grandmama takes her two o'clock nap. Previously, when Grandmama asked what I was writing about at school, I'd give her generic terms: parenthood (versus parenting as a Brown woman in the South), family (versus generational trauma), and history (versus the role of Asians in race relations). Grandmama is strong-willed and opinionated like me, or like I used to be, so it is not worth either of our time delving into our respective concerns, because it took a while—almost four years—for us to be at peace with one another. Now we are each other's helpers. She sends me money for diapers and groceries, I repay her with news about her grandchildren and great-grandchildren. On most visits, too, I arrange her dishes, coffee pot, supplements, and newspaper where she can pat around for them without knocking them off the shelves or counter. I leave zippered bags of pumpkin minimuffins for her midmorning snack, all bite-size to keep her sugar intake in check and to keep her from needing a fork or a knife.

She congratulates me as we sit down to talk about the grandchildren and the great-grandchildren. *You obtained yourself a master's degree, I declare. I reckon the first master of writing in the family.*

We proceed with the usual: Cousin E is having another baby, sister-in-law J is also having one—both boys. Cousin A is now working for an insurance company, and our little girl, whom we often call Bitty, enjoyed her first year at preschool. But Grandmama is neither listening to me nor looking at me. She is staring at the blue IKEA bag at my feet. My ears and neck get hot. I am nervous thinking about what she might discover should she dig through my pile. She moves from the rocking chair to the couch where I am sitting, leans forward, and reaches down. All of me freezes, and I can hear my heartbeat in my ear. Her fingers unfurl from a fist and stretch toward the bag, lower and lower, to the floor, to my thoughts and musings and secrets, until they finally furl again, not around the corner of a book or a folder, but around the bag handle that spells out in yellow: I-K-E-A.

Now what is this bag? It's a mighty fine bag, she says, feeling the polypropylene like the forehead of a grandchild. *So big.*

It is, Grandmama. It's the biggest bag I own, I say. I call the dog over to distract her and ask her if she likes the dog's summer haircut. But she doesn't mind the dog. He patters away. She keeps touching the outside of the bag.

And this bag can hold wet things?

I tell her the bag is made of polypropylene, that it is waterproof. Her eyes smile. She asks what the word on the handle means, and I tell her IKEA is the name of the store I purchased it from. But I don't tell her that my family frequented IKEA when we first moved to the United States—the only store we could afford to buy furniture from, the only kind of furniture that could fit in the two small rooms split between thirteen of us, and where we treated ourselves to one-dollar cinnamon buns.

She doesn't say anything more but keeps feeling the bag, crinkling the material, smoothing her hand across the seams, and testing her grip on the short handle, then the long handle. I can tell she's coveting the dollar-fifty sack, so I walk to the pantry to retrieve a few garbage bags and begin transferring my books, folders, and manuscript into them. *It's yours, Grandmama. I know you'll put it to good use.*

The bag is perfect for her arthritis, knees, and near-blindness. The handles are softer and gentler than those of a wicker basket. The long handle means she could hang it from her shoulder while she emptied it of the clothes that she was hanging over the line. The polypropylene catches the water, which means the laundry can't drench her clothes as they hang from her side—pneumonia is a senior citizen's worst enemy. And because she can't see very well and is prone to fall, the bag dangling by her side means she won't trip over it on the ground, and therefore won't crack her skull or break her hip in the middle of her portion of

Purefield's meadows. I know now what my role, or one of my roles, in Grandmama's life is: to bring her news along with simple technology, to not only keep her up-to-date with the goings-on of the world but also to bring small joys into what I imagine is a lonely life in an empty house built by her late husband, a life of sunup to sundown with no one to hum old hymns to but herself.

In the coming months, I will bring her a four-by-four-inch photo magnet that fits the square-format pictures she now receives from grandchildren—Instagram-style photos. I will also bring her the cherry-pistachio tart from the French patisserie I work at in Charleston—something to satiate her sweet tooth but that has a lower sugar and preservative content than her usual Little Debbies—and a highlighter with a clicker so she can highlight verses in her Bible and captions in the newspaper without losing the cap and having to bend down to find it or worse, slipping on it. When I notice that her dog looks suddenly old and unwell, I take a picture of him and print it. I hold on to the picture until he passes, mail the photograph to Grandmama, and write a note that says: *Something to remember Bucky by. He loved you.*

———

I have no heirloom. I have nothing to go back to. I have nothing to pass on.

The houses I've lived in are now extinct due to fire or foreclosure and becoming condemned, eventually demolished. I now consider the memories from these houses endangered, and I write to preserve them. The same is true for anything else I might have owned as a child or a teen. I came to America as an unaccompanied minor awaiting adoption, aboard a trans-Pacific flight, with only a duffel bag and a pair of Tretorn sneakers to my then name. Once adopted, I moved out of my sister's two-bedroom dwelling and lived in a large house on a prissy part of Long Island, which is now also just a memory—maybe it's just my fate. The new owners have remodeled it to the point of keeping nothing but the curb appeal. Once a young adult able to survive in Manhattan, I subleased for weeks or months at a time. The last New York apartment I lived in housed me for two years—which, per my record, is a very long time. Because I moved frequently, I lived with little, my belongings all fitting in a duffel bag, a suitcase, and a granny cart. I slept on an air mattress until I got married. I didn't own furniture.

Perhaps this is why, when I visit Grandmama's house, I have to touch every mantelpiece and table, sit in every seat, open every cupboard, smell the decades-old potpourri. I work my hands into the contents of every basket, whether it is a basket of toys or a basket of quilting cloths. I ask S what each piece of farm equipment is called, I read the newspaper clippings Grandmama has taped to a cabinet door, and I read the books. I feel gratitude for the sense of permanence here, but sometimes the permanence gives me—I don't know what else to call it—a fright.

———

We evacuate to Purefield, the way we do every year when big storms come. Grandmama doesn't have internet, and the cable is unreliable, the cell phone signal spotty. Dust has settled on most things, and there's a hornet's nest on the kitchen window that I'm bothered by but can't do anything about. I grow bored and anxious; I feel trapped. I read. I can read a book from the stash I've brought with me, but instead I start with a ledger from Grandmama's library, a record of farm activity. The first entry is from 1969 and notes the sale of calves: when, for how much, to whom. The calves have funny names: Big 122, Pee Wee, Shag, Big Teat. They sound like names of rappers from the '90s, and I laugh. The calves' sires have equally comical names but with heft to them: Carl the Cow, Amigo, King Rafter, King Byron the Great. Every cow has a number, digits corresponding to a tag stapled to an ear, declaring each mammal as property. The ledger goes on like this for pages, detailing cow sales through the late '70s. After these lists, the pages contain a scatter of information: the weather, the kind of feed purchased and distributed, farm helpers' names and their driver's license numbers, the sex of each cow, the number of hay bales trucked in. Some pages list tools or supplies purchased for the month. For example, in June 1970: eight sheets of plywood, twelve window lights, a four-foot metal door and frame, two door locks, and a gallon of white outdoor paint. Sporadically, the writer notes names of visitors, a grocery list, and an address to send a collection bill to.

The handwriting is Grandmama's—I recognize it from the notecards she's sent me, each one ending with a Psalm. The itemization in the ledger I also recognize as being hers. She writes the same way she talks—no breaks, no edits, more note-taking than composition. Some pages have newspaper clippings stapled or paper clipped to them, and I *know* how religiously Grandmama clips stories from papers and magazines. I say *Wow* to myself: her notebooks are a memoirist's or essayist's dream: every detail noted, every memory preserved for later use. I then wonder why she's recorded such minutiae, what she has done or hopes to do with the information.

I close the ledger and flip through another book, and there I find prose by voluble authors, more minutiae, chatter. As mute as S's family is in real life, I discover that they are loose-tongued on paper. On the page, they say everything: their virtues and their sins. On the page, they sound animate, move in each setting dynamically, paint a world in vivid colors. When they write about the Queen Anne's lace, they write about it as though it were real lace as opposed to a noxious weed.

I stop reading when my daughter comes into the room to ask if she can go with her daddy's cousin to feed the cows and say goodbye to the calves. The family will sell the calves from the half year at a sale tomorrow, and my daughter thinks she is only saying goodbye to them because they will be moving to a different home. We don't tell her that they will be veal, that they will be killed. I particularly do not mention that the brown-black one, the one she hand-feeds grass to and sings Bruno Mars songs to, will eat his last meal tonight and mosey onto the trailer that will drive him to his death.

———

I am here again, tired of evacuating to this place every time a hurricane hits.

I sit in bed surrounded by the family's books. Beyond my reach, more literature about my husband's family. And beyond there, open space—so open it feels like nature is trying to overawe to the point of quashing. Aunt Julia has long passed, and with her the only bit of levity in this place has gone. I complain now of headaches when S brings me here, as if the air or the foliage or the attitude in Purefield is a natural cause for cephalalgia. I go about my days with sleepy eyes no matter how much walking or cleaning I do to wake myself up. I resort to staying in bed to read, because reading sinks me into the thoughts of somebody else and I can forget about my discomfort. S takes our daughter to see the cows, then to play with cousins down the road.

My reading takes me to 1700s Purefield, when the first of the line settled here, drove out the Catawba and Cherokee, and built a fort to protect their daughters from what the books call *savages*. The books then take me to the 1800s, when the Clarsons fashioned original machinery not unlike Eli Whitney's cotton gin and when they owned slaves, some purchased for around $1,000 for the specific use of breeding more help—enslaved babymakers, or what the author of one of the diaries depicts as something like a rollover investment. I read about the segregated schools of the early 1900s, and about the pride with which Weis Academy, the local private school, was founded after Brown v. Board. I hate what I am learning, so I read more. I am the protagonist now; they are the bad guys.

I devour what Grandmama's shelves offer me. I read for hours—through lunch, which I, like most Filipinos, have never missed. I copy quotes from the texts into my notebook. I now know more about this family than anybody else does, including my husband. But maybe not Grandmama, I can't be sure. I write the notes because writing helps commit to memory what I might later on use in an essay or conversation or argument. I take pictures of paragraphs with my phone.

Nearing dinnertime, I take a break to make food. My daughter helps with making the rolls. She tells me about the cows as she forms thawed-out dough into crescents. *What did you do today?* she and S ask, and I tell them that all I've done is read and that I plan to get back into it after we eat. *Mama, please come with us tomorrow.* Night falls, bedtime songs are sung. I return to the prose.

The next morning, I wake up asking myself why, in recent visits, I spend hours in bed to read about the family. No longer convinced that my headaches are the reason, and admitting to myself that they are psychosomatic, I take the headaches as more of an effect than a cause. Why do I read? Why does my brain tell my head to throb when we are here? Why do I withdraw from the pastures and seclude myself in a room scattered with the family's tomes? I can say that it is a way to get to know my husband, but I know that I can learn more by spending time with him. I can go to the barns and have him teach me how to feed the animals. I can let him show me the creek or the pool where he learned how to cannonball and dive, the dirt path where he ran as a child. Instead, I stay in this room, collecting information about his heritage. I study the county that birthed his grandmother and mother, and I look at where, in the line stretching from Adam to him, I might have a place, a connection. I keep looking. I find nothing.

Maybe I amass these stories—about heroes and antiheroes—to tally how many times I am better and they are worse. For years, a good number of these relatives made me feel like I was an intruder, an insult, my husband's betrayal. But here, counterevidence.

I roll out from under S's arm and get out of bed. I wash my face. In the mirror, I see a brown-skinned girl with black hair, a small nose, full lips. I see body language acquired over the past few years: a nervous, constant tucking of hair behind ears. The house still quiet, I think of the conversations I might have today. I will tell Grandmama more of the same: who is engaged, who is pregnant, and which big company is moving into Charleston and bringing in hundreds of jobs—Grandmama is ever so concerned about Carolinians having jobs. But I will not tell her that along with the rapid development of the city, they are taking down Confederate flags and certain monuments, that in a sea of Republican red, Charleston is an expanding blue dot.

My daughter will ask me to come see the cows again, and I will make up another excuse about work or chores or my headache. I will not tell her that I don't go out to the pastures and to the barns because I feel so alien there. Pastures, barns: they contain language I didn't grow up speaking, equipment I can't name, people who will avoid eye contact. I will not tell my daughter that I tried to love this place for its Queen Anne's lace, for the fresh air, the space to write, but that the forced appreciation summoned nothing true. I will not tell her that I don't go out there because out there is only loneliness and quiet, and in here, with the books, something feels familiar and safe. The books, the authors and characters, at least speak. I will not tell her that I tried to love this place for her and for her father, but I am growing weary now. Maybe I should tell someone—maybe my husband. When we drive off the interstate and I see the pines, I have to count my breaths and listen to them. When we step into the farmhouse and all I hear are our dog's toenails clacking against the floor, my mouth dries. When I first came here, I wore a tuxedo shirt and heels. I rarely come here with anything other than sweatpants now.

I splash my face again. I brush my teeth. I fold down the toilet seat cover and sit. And I stay there, in the nothing, in that part of the life I did agree to live.

———

I am folding laundry in the den, on the couch where Aunt Julia sat when I first met her, on our fifth night of evacuation at the farmhouse. It's become our longest stay here; the Category 4 storm won't keep a predictable path, and the governor has not lifted the evacuation order. I'm nearly out of our rations, and I refuse to feed my child the white bread and noodle packets in Grandmama's pantry. I never know how long ago she bought groceries.

I say to S as he walks in from the kitchen, *Please take us to Greenville tomorrow. We're almost out of food.*

He mutters something that I can't hear.

Oh god, speak up! I can't hear you! I can never hear you. I don't transition, I just switch—from at ease to angry.

He takes a breath and tries again. He walks over so I can hear him better and says with the same low, defeated voice that he's wary of driving in the storm, since it could hit from anywhere, bring in a tornado, make a tree fall. I tell him I need to see sidewalks and buildings, people. And he says to wait, it's safer if we do. I fold the clothes faster, with swift, sharp movements that do nothing but rumple the clothes. He sits down by me, refolds what I've fumbled, breathes audibly. I don't want to hear his breaths. I want to hear his thoughts. Peeved, I move to the rocking chair. He keeps folding the clothes even when I've stopped, and I am rocking back and forth so aggressively, the chair has slid off the rug. I force the chair to creak, as if to speak the family's language of passivity—the rocking chair's creaking longhand for *I resent everything here.* He finishes folding and transfers the clothes into IKEA bags, and

I only see him do this through my peripheral vision. I refuse to look at him. I withhold.

I know, he says.

I wait to see if he'll complete his thought. I fix my eyes on the digital clock atop Grandmama's newspapers, count the minutes before another sound drawls out of him. Four minutes.

I know that I've devastated you. He cries. I have seen my husband cry only thrice in the decade we've known each other: once in college, in exasperation, when he was telling me about his past, another time with more joyful tears when he watched me walk down the aisle to him, and the last time was when our daughter was born. Each previous time he'd cried without sound, displaying emotion through such a strong grimace, it might have hurt his face. This time, he sniffs, shakes a little. His voice is altered by his attempt at not letting tears flow. But he talks and I can't get a word in. I'm not sure I want to. He says he's well aware of the sadness of this place, how lonely it must be for me—an outsider who married someone who also feels like an outsider. He says that it kills him to know that here, I talk, but without the freedom to speak about topics that interest me. That here, I alter my speech, my intonation, my code, my voice. He knows how much I miss my family, how much they talk, how loud, how fierce, how passionate they are. How conversations don't always end with a resolution, but they always, *always*, end with a snack. He feels this void, too. He misses my culture, too.

I know that he knows that I know more about this family than he does, from what I've read, been told, or overheard. He says that he doesn't know how I endure, how I force myself to stay silent in front of all that is unsaid and swept under the rug: what happened to Julia, to Margaret, to husbands and wives and children, to the sons at the dinner table that late night in the 1960s, to Grandmama after her brother died, after her husband died, and what she did and said after someone came to her to tell their truth. *Maybe we all know,* he says. Maybe everyone knows about what has transpired on this land, the details of their heritage, the source of the guilt with which they wake up and go to bed, the trauma, and maybe that is why they don't talk. If only the barns and silos could speak. Maybe they thought silence is the best cover-up, that silence is the only salve. He says they were wrong, that it's done nothing but bring more pain. *I'm used to it, but you're not. I don't know how you absorb all of it without going crazy.* He slumps forward and holds his head in his hands.

I want to comfort him, but I'm not ready to seal him up. I want him to keep talking. I've been drowning in the quiet; I enjoy the fight. When he talks, I can believe that he understands my loss. Is it not one of the points of marriage—to carry each other's burdens? To feel together?

I say, *Then why do we come here? Why betray me this way?* It takes another four minutes for him to speak. I grow impatient, but waiting worked last time, so I let him be. I clench the rocking chair's armrests.

As much as I feel like I don't belong here, and neither do you, there are the cousins, tire swings, nature. I know what he means. He means the things sold to us as the makings of a happy childhood: fresh air, skipping stones, chases through the woods, farm animals to pet and feed.

I take my time to respond, hold him captive in the quiet. I let my thoughts trail off to quotes and passages in my head, and I think of two writers who have guided me: Joan Didion, who wrote about coming home for the promise of cousins and rivers and uncombed hair and picnics by the stream and how marriage was a kind of betrayal, and Bharati Mukherjee, whose novel's protagonist, an Indian immigrant, escaped trauma, fled to America, and found her love and true self in New York but was forced into a desolate farm life in Iowa. I ask him, speaking softer this time, as if we're lying down pillow to pillow, if he remembers me reading these stories out loud to him when I was in graduate school. He nods. He tells me that he knew why I had read them to him, what I was trying to say, but the call of the country was strong—especially when I, an immigrant who had lost everything once before, offered nothing to counteract Purefield's tout and lure. He asks,

If we don't come here, and if we have nowhere else to go when it storms, when we're sick or injured, or when it's the holidays, what would we do and where would we go? Would we just be untethered, be without history or geography? Will we sustain?

Well, this place surely doesn't sustain.

He shakes his head in agreement. I tell him we can at least try to go for long periods of not coming here, to afford ourselves time to reboot, learn our limitations, establish rules. I quote my therapist: I say that we can walk away from the places and things that are unhealthy for us, or that we can draw parameters that set what is allowed and what isn't. He pitches in ideas, and clearly now, I see that he's been plotting ways out of here, too. He suggests we save money for more frequent trips to New York, perhaps even for a passport for me. We joke about evacuating to the Great Wolf Lodge next time a hurricane hits, or camping in the mountains—a hobby neither one of us really knows about. He gets up to walk to the kitchen, and I worry that this is the end of our exchange. But he comes back into the den with two glasses and a bottle of Knob Creek he's been hiding from Grandmama. He pours some. We continue to talk through the night, in various tones and inflections, with mannerisms slight and big but that all belong to, and are representative of, the multitudes that live within us, that have found no room nor match nor value here. We talk and we talk. Our voices eclipse the night.

———

It is October, hurricane season once again, and I have avoided Grandmama since presidential candidates were announced. It is the longest stretch we've had not seeing each other since S "brought home a girl from New York." And now we are back at the clotheslines, where Grandmama has hung white sheets, lights, and delicates. We park our car near the wall of white and off-white fabric, and the sensor Cousin R installed in the driveway alerts Grandmama that visitors are here. But we are less like visitors and more like evacuees today, with Hurricane Matthew slamming hard against the coast. I had planned on staying put in our second-floor condo, believing it to be untouchable by the flood, but my friends persuaded me to pack up and leave. They said the last time a hurricane of this magnitude hit the Lowcountry, it took down a bridge, and the barrier islands and peninsula were without power and water for weeks. Hotels up the highway are fully booked, and Airbnb leaves us with only a $300-per-night option. Everyone wanted to avoid a deathly storm, and I simply wanted to avoid Grandmama's opinions on the elections.

I'm so glad y'all made it here. Fox says that this storm will kill everybody, she tells us as she steps out of the back door.

I look down so she can't see me roll my eyes. *Hi, Grandmama. I'm sure it won't* kill *everybody.*

Y'all been busy now, haven't you? I haven't seen you in a while.

Just workin' hard, ma'am, S says.

I nudge him to go ahead and go inside without me, and I make a hand sign that looks like a talking bird, instructing him to do the talking today—because I won't be doing it. I tell our daughter she can stay behind and help shepherd the dog while I unload the car. I take my time, I unpack and repack bags in the trunk. But the wind picks up and the clouds roll in. We go inside.

In the house, I don't sit so that I'm not stationary long enough for Grandmama to spot me and situate herself by me. I keep busy with putting away groceries, setting up a coloring station for my girl, and filling a bowl of water for the dog. I am scolding the dog for jumping, when I smell something burning. I walk to the stove to check, and there sits a saucepan with burnt pieces of carrot sitting in hot oil. I turn the burner off, grab a dish towel to hold the pan's handle with, take the pan, and fling it into the sink.

This could've burned down your house, Grandmama!

Well, the Lord sent you here to stop it.

I look down and roll my eyes again. She pats me on the back like she always does when she approves of something I've done or said, walks to the television, and turns it on. Fox News is on and it's loud, and I want to be back in our home, in the middle of the hurricane that will supposedly kill everybody. As I scrub the scorched saucepan, S puts an arm around my shoulders and whispers, *This is going to be fun—not.* And we shake our heads and giggle. I keep scrubbing, and he turns around to set the table for lunch.

The television stays on through lunch: exchanges between Fox studio anchors and meteorologists onsite in Florida and the Carolina coast. They keep repeating that everybody will die, and only interrupt this banter with praise for Donald Trump and accusations against Hillary Clinton. But I suppose that having this babel in the background is better than turning off the television and having to make conversation with Grandmama. So we sit through it until our plates are empty, and I can busy myself again with a task. I take the dishes to the sink and begin scrubbing, and then I notice that the TV volume has decreased.

Grandmama walks back into the kitchen like the Clarson matriarch that she is, suddenly strong in the bones and unaffected by arthritis. She is queen again; even my daughter, who is coloring on the floor, feels a change in the air. We look to where she is standing, and she is towering over the dining table and holding on to one of the chairs like it's a cane, a scepter. She says, without introduction or preface, *Y'all better tell me who y'all are voting for.*

I blink hard. Standing over the sink, I turn off the water and look out the window. The whites and off-whites on the clotheslines are billowing in the wind.

I have an easy way out of the trap. *I'm just a permanent resident, not a citizen. Can't vote, Grandmama.*

But who do you think of voting for?

S walks in from the bedroom. *Ma'am, I think it's best if we talk about something else.*

Tell me.

Grandmama, S says as he gathers crayons from the floor, *I don't want to talk about this.* He guides our daughter to the other room.

Trump's a good man. You're from farmers and you know he'll help farmers.

I snap. *He might, but he likely won't. Do you really believe all that he says, Grandmama?*

Well, do y'all believe that we should let outsiders into this country?

I know she's referring to refugees because the topic has been all over the news.

Yes, Grandmama, I say, now turning away from the window and toward her. *S and I helped to relocate a family of six from the Congo. The youngest one is just a year old, and she probably hasn't had a good meal in a while.*

Y'all know they could be terrorists!

A baby? A terrorist? A single mother of five?

She goes on for a good five minutes about strangers entering this land and ravaging it with their different ways and their different customs and their religions. She goes on for another five lecturing us about how her daddy and her daddy's daddy tilled this soil we're standing on, and how they built this house and farmed this land, and that she would hate to see another take it from her.

I tell her, *This land? This land that belonged to the Catawba and the Cherokee? C'mon, Grandmama, who really took from whom? Purefield? This was Catawba and Cherokee country. People lived here before your people did.*

This belongs to us.

This belonged to someone else for seven thousand years. And your family didn't till this soil. Enslaved people did.

Colored people can't claim to have done nothin'.

Grandmama! S walks back in and raises his voice slightly. *You have to stop calling them that. You can't talk about people like that.*

Y'all just trust anybody.

I know what she's insinuating—this is the narrative, the lie, they keep telling themselves in this part of the state: that Black men are unsafe, especially to White women.

Grandmama! S and I bellow together.

We go back and forth about immigrants and people of color and slavery, S chiming in just as quickly as I am.

Grandmama says that "colored" people and mixed children don't fare well, and I tell her that I hope she realizes that her great-grandchild, who is coloring in the next room, is mixed and is faring pretty well in life. I tell her the best and smartest people I know are descendants of enslaved men and women, are immigrants, are mixed, are all shades of Brown. She tells me that America belongs to Americans, and I ask if she means White. I also ask her to clarify whether or not that is the reason she couldn't accept me at first, and she says, after stuttering a bit, that it was more because I was undocumented—*illegal.*

There's no way of tellin' if you were marrying S for your visa.

I tell her that if that's what I wanted to do, I would've married someone in New York and not have left my family and friends. I would've found someone in a city of eight million people, and not here, not in a town where there's more cattle than humans. I remind her that she gossiped about me with cousins and neighbors and aunts, that when I came down to meet everyone during our engagement, I could feel their animosity seep through their teeth and eyes. I remind her that she told them I was dangerous, trouble. I tell her that I am trouble, that I will rock this family and all of Purefield County. I will tell the stories. I have never spoken back to her this way, but I'm letting it all out.

And Grandmama, who brings you food and gadgets? Who comes here to bring you news? Who has the patience to sit through your stories and litanies? Is it not me? Did I not just save your house from burning down?

It was different then, she says. *I didn't know you.*

I didn't know you *and I didn't think anything bad of you.* I tell her she only doesn't know people because she's here in this empty house, in the middle of this farm, listening to no one but her television.

She doesn't say anything but she whimpers. There are no tears, but she makes whistling sounds like the wind is making outside, the blusters blowing from the coast to the upcountry, the gusts feeding into the pines and softening just slightly when they reach the meadows. I imagine the sparrows and barred owls taking shelter, the deer following along, the pine cones crackling to open up. My daughter comes back into the kitchen with a crayon in her hand and inches closer to me until she can melt into my side. I wing her under my arm.

Let's pack up, I say.

Hold up now, the queen finally speaks. *I don't want y'all to leave. I don't want y'all to leave thinking I don't love y'all. I love you.* She's looking at my daughter. *And I love* you. She's looking at me. *I pray for all my grandchildren and their spouses every night. But you, you're the smartest one. You have the words for everything, I'm so proud of your writing.*

Grandmama, you don't even know what I write about. Everything I said just a minute ago, I write about all that stuff. You proud of that?

I am. I just don't know. I don't know. But you have to know that I love you.

I walk around to her side of the table and hug her neck, so tight that I might strangle her. I hold it there until she attempts to speak again, then I let go. I start to pack up by picking up the dog's bowl, then the leftover crayons on the floor. Grandmama doesn't move during the ten minutes it takes for us to pack up our things and gather them at the door. S steps outside first, then our daughter and our dog. I exit last and Grandmama stops me.

I'm sorry.

I'm sorry for you, too, Grandmama. I pull the door shut.

We drive away, and the sound of gravel crushing under the tires is comforting—they are making the sound that I thought I heard

Grandmama's thoughts make during my rebutting. I smile a little. We pull farther and farther away on the road, past clearings where who knows how many enslaved people worked and died; the clearings where the ancient people of this land buried their beloveds. We drive past the church the Clarsons call Salvation, where tombstones bear significant family names: Damien, Dustin Pritchett, Damien Roy, Esther, Richard, Richard Jr. They bear names of farmers, hatmakers, home doctors, soldiers, Klansmen. I look back to see the stones sprouting from the graves, lives and deaths and legacies this town only speaks of on paper. I remember that there is a paid-for lot for my in-laws here. I remember that S has asked if I wanted to be buried here one day, too. I finally have an answer to this question from long ago, and yes, I'll join the Clarsons here. I'll pay for the lot. I'll design a headstone: a marker in the shape of an eight-rayed sun, the Philippine emblem, painted in the jewel tones of my islands. The epitaph will say: *Married into this family and told stories—stories that dragged them out of their fiction.*

The Gulf Between,
the War Within

2016

We talk but we don't talk. This is what's been between us for over twenty years. Two decades since he left the house, our family, me. I was eight, fifteen, twenty. Now I am thirty, a mother, a journalist. Today, what is supposed to be the last day of winter, I sit down with my papa at my sister's house on Long Island so I can write about our events and people, our cause and effect, the Gulf War of 1990, the war that drained my parents of the post-Spanish wealth my mother inherited and the post-American money that afforded my father first-class flights, hotel suites, and a mansion on the outskirts of Manila. The Gulf War was our deluge, the storm that brought down everything, the reason why I named my memoir *Monsoon Mansion*. Now I do what journalists do: interview. We talk about the storm.

Papa is sitting on the couch across from me, and I'm on the settee. Between us is an ottoman where I've rested the voice recorder. I wear a baseball cap to hold my hair but also to hide my face. "I'm a journalist, not your daughter," I say, as I press the red button on the recorder. I ask him to state his name, age, location, and the date. I tell him his volume is good but he needs to enunciate, and then, "Okay, ready."

"Why did you leave?" I finally ask. Even though what I really want to ask is why did he leave *me*.

He talks and I leave it to the voice recorder to listen. My mind is back in our house in Manila, at the top of the stairs where he said goodbye.

"It was a good plan," he says about his initial efforts to recruit Filipinos for employment in oil sites, plants, and hotels in Kuwait, Saudi Arabia, Jordan, and the Emirates. "Our people needed jobs." Between 1979 and 1990, Papa brought tens of thousands of under- and unemployed men from the islands to feed the Gulf with the labor force it needed to develop cities and dig for oil. He recruited them for a middleman's fee, and brought them over village by village. He connected Arab entrepreneurship with the diligence and, as the employers called it, relative docility of Filipinos. He fought for better work conditions at the plants; for more comfortable beds, thicker blankets, ventilation inside barracks. He set up phone stations so workers could call home. He had it, and they had it, good for eleven years.

Then Iraq invaded Kuwait, and the United States got involved, forming a coalition of thirty-nine nations. I remember watching footage on CNN with Papa, scenes of explosions and automatic gunfire from cameras mounted on American bombers. My brother and I likened the siege to our Nintendo video games, the closeness of the camera to the onslaught and the closeness of our faces to the screen.

Papa says he left us because it was the only way he could save his workers from the effects of the war. When the war broke out, he says, 63,000 Filipinos were displaced out of their workers' barracks and forced to wander in the desert, hide in camps, search for food, pray for water. Papa spent five hundred dollars to resettle each returning worker, totaling more than thirty million dollars from his personal checking and savings accounts, stocks, liquidated assets, and borrowed funds. Between August 1990 and March 1991, about 30,000 Filipinos were repatriated by him and local agencies. He says, "But what about the other 33,000? What about them? Nobody cared! Only *I* wanted to save them."

Then he quotes headlines he remembers. He says that the Philippine government sent only 161 flights to the Gulf. "Do the math," Papa says. "If an average jet can fit 250 passengers, how many—*how few*—can 161 flights hold?" I do the math on my steno. But I do it not because I'm interested in the figures, though I should be, but because I don't want to look Papa in the eye. He leans forward, as if to make sure that the recorder doesn't miss the next part. He talks straight into it like I'm not there, like I was never there, and recounts who he had to contact to rally support for worker repatriation. I remember this part. I used to sit at his feet, playing with my Rollerblade Barbie, while he dialed the hotline number for the Philippine Overseas Employment Administration, or POEA, on the rotary phone, while he begged for the other person not to hang up.

Papa repatriated nearly half of his workers, but the fight didn't end there. Once they got back, they couldn't find jobs or couldn't recover from the trauma. During the first month of rescue, 16,500 Filipinos returned home, but only one hundred of them secured employment. Those who were able to stuff their pockets, shoes, and underwear with Arab money brought home worthless currency—the central bank stopped its Arab currency exchange operations.

Papa left the summer I turned eight so he could, I know now, find new revenue streams in Niigata, Japan, and developing island towns south of Manila. He deserted us and the mansion so he could travel to where there were investors and where his new ideas—fishing net technology and efficient farm irrigation—could become another million-dollar venture. He also left because the emotional toll of a wife who blamed him for the downfall was too much to carry along with the burden of repatriating thousands of Filipino citizens. He disappeared from my life until I was twelve, then he remarried and got his footing back in Manila, but he never asked me back to live with him. Instead he sent me off to live with my oldest sister.

Papa says, after glancing at me, "There were reports of Iraqi soldiers raping stranded Filipino women."

I am not hearing the answer I want. Twenty years I waited, not for data, news reports, or shocking headlines, but for answers to the questions I've been dying to ask: *Why did you leave? Do you know what happened to us after you left the house? Do you know what we had to go through?*

2002

I am in the car with my uncle, Tito Eric, stuck in the usual Manila traffic. He is my favorite ride to school because he always has stories that give insight into my father's otherworld—headscarves, dusty brows and beards, men working under the hot Arabian sun, their shoes filling up with just-as-hot desert sand. He was one of my father's first recruits to the Middle East, and they worked together to build the barracks, canteens, and phone stations my father loved to boast about. Tito Eric is quiet except in the car, when he is clutching at the steering wheel, looking at the road, talking to someone but talking to no one. He asks if it's okay that he smokes, rolls his window down and taps his cigarette, and he recalls: The day the Gulf War broke out and he stuffed his clothes with cash, his sweat dampening the stash. That evening when, after many evenings without food, water, and protection from windstorms and the sun, he helped bury a friend in an unmarked grave. That time he finally crossed from Kuwait to Jordan, got through all checkpoints, got a seat on a rescue plane and slept the whole flight home, only to wake up to the realization that there were no jobs in the islands—which was why he had left in the first place. He works for us now; he's a relative who is paid to drive me to and from school, soccer practice, or a school soiree. Papa promised him employment, and this is how he could deliver on that promise. When he switched industries— from labor recruitment to construction—Papa regained some portion of the wealth he lost during the Gulf War, and when he could, he gave returning workers jobs.

Tito Eric lights another cigarette. "Don't ever take up smoking," he tells me. "This is for those of us who have sad stories." I don't mind him smoking, but I mind that he keeps saying he has sad stories. I mind because, right now, he is the closest thing I have to a father. I see him more than I see Papa, even though Papa is back in Manila. Tito Eric knows my friends and the boy I meet up with under the sky bridge, and he knows my jersey number. He sits through every game, smoking on the sidelines, and he cheers me on, wheezing.

2016

Papa has a stroke two weeks after the interview. I fly to New York at 4:00 a.m. I cry at the check-in kiosk, through TSA, and while board- ing. My sister texts before I put my phone on airplane mode: HAVE YOU LEFT? DOC SAYS HE MAY OR MAY NOT MAKE IT.

I make it to LaGuardia, then to NYU Winthrop Hospital's ICU. My sister hugs me and says, "He's inside." I walk into the curtained-off room where my father breathes from a tank. He opens his eyes when I step closer, like he's ready to talk—to talk more, to *really* talk.

He says, "Read to me what you wrote from our interview."

I sit down in the chair next to the bed and pull out my laptop from my backpack. I open the seventh chapter from the memoir I'd been working on, and I read. He doesn't interrupt, doesn't ask ques- tions, doesn't object or agree. My eyes are glossy by the chapter's last paragraph, and still, he says nothing. The chapter ends and he asks me to read the preceding ones, the pages that introduce readers to our life before the Gulf War: the parties, the bedtime stories, the poolside picnics. The only sounds in our part of the ICU are my reading and his heart rate monitor's beeping. We put a pause on story time so he can eat his lunch of mashed potato and peas, and while he eats, I fall asleep in the hospital chair.

I wake up and it is almost midnight, and the nurses have wheeled him in and out of the room twice. He has had an MRI and his catheter replaced, the nurse tells me. She also tells me that my father is very talkative. "So many stories. You're lucky he can still talk after his stroke." Then she asks if I mind giving him a sponge bath, or if she should do it herself. I say I can do it, it's the least I can do, convinced that my interview, my interrogation, my culling of the past, were the cause of his stroke. I take the washcloth, soap, and basin from the nurse and proceed to wash my father. He says, "Read more. Read to the end."

And I read through all the chapters I've written as I give my father a sponge bath. It is the closest we've been since he hugged me and said goodbye at the top of the mansion's stairs when I was eight. I read from the laptop, which rests on the same hospital cart that holds the basin of soapy water. I read about the times when I had no food or water, my father having left so he could provide food and water to those stranded in the war. I read about what happened to the mansion, what and who it housed, what I had to endure while my father saved his men.

In the book, I never say that my father abandoned us. I say that he left to rescue his workers. In the book, I never call it absence, nor desertion, nor neglect. I use the words *distance* and *loss*. I paint it as though he was the savior for 63,000 men, but I never say that we were the sacrifice, the offering, or in war terms, the collateral damage.

When I finish, he says, "You're too nice."

And this is the answer I've been waiting for—assurance that my father knew all along how many birthdays, soccer games, campouts he missed; that we lost him so he wouldn't lose his men. That we needed a hero, too.

I cannot stand the transparency, this new clarity. It is not the language of our family. I fold my laptop closed and fit it back into my backpack. I sling the straps over one shoulder and walk to the door.

My father asks, "Where are you going?"

"Downstairs for a smoke."

"But you don't smoke."

"No, I don't."

"Don't smoke. Cigarettes killed your Tito Eric."

"The smoking didn't," I say. "The sad stories did."

Why Your Mother Can't Drive

Dear Malaya,

Your mother can't drive, so she takes you from place to place on a yellow bike. When you were smaller, you rode in an attached bike trailer with a five-point harness. Now you ride straddling the padded rectangle on the rear rack, on a cushion made of your mother's old scarves. You rest your helmeted head on the curve just below your mother's nape, wrap your arms around her waist, and she pedals.

Her speed: twelve miles per hour. Your comfort: the smell of sweat off her back.

Your mother can't drive, so she and your father have bought a condo in what the realtor called "a walking neighborhood." Your school, the urgent care clinic, the post office, the supermarket, the bakery, the dentist, the CVS with a full pharmacy, the skate park, the dog park, the community pool, the soccer field, the one Filipino friend who speaks your mother's language, the café where she writes, the salad place where she meets her writing students and clients, and the bar your parents whisk off to when Mimi is in town to watch you—they're all within a two-mile radius.

Your world: this circle. Her world: life on two wheels.

Your mother can't drive, so she can't chaperone field trips, can't pick you up with a gang of friends for an after-school playdate, can't queue up in the carpool line. She parks her bike behind the bush outside your classroom, waves at you from the other side of the gravel parking lot, and signals to you when it's safe to cross. "Is that your mom's bike? Are you biking home with your mom?" your friends ask most days. "So cool." But when it rains, the other moms roll down their windows and say, "Y'all need a ride?" Your mother refuses, always. "No thanks," she says and zips up your rain jacket, then hers.

Your protection from the afternoon showers: a shell of pink, heart-print waterproof material. Her shell: having survived poverty, hunger, an abusive mother and stepfather, a monsoon, a deteriorating mansion, and the belief that she doesn't need anybody's help.

Your mother can't drive, so when you forget your project at home, she bikes just slightly faster—thirteen miles per hour on second gear without slowing down at speed humps—and balances the two-foot-wide and one-foot-tall cardboard installation on the bike handle, clamping it with the inner sides of her arms and holding it down with her chin. She says "fuck" when the chopstick antenna piece falls off and "fuck" again when the scotch-taped sign that says *Counting to 100* gets blown away by the wind she's cycling against. She parks the bike on the curb and searches for your handiwork, and when she finds the chopstick under a bush and the crayoned sign in the gutter, she dusts them off with the back of her hand and holds them with her teeth before she mounts the bike again. She rides like this, trying not to slobber. She arrives at the school, and your teacher meets her at the front door, lets her in, asks what she's brought with her, and when she replies, your teacher says, "Oh, it's for Thursday. Not today." So she bikes back home and does it again, your project trapped under the weight of her chin and the weight of her invisible handicap, and again on Thursday, when the project is actually due.

Your words: *I'm sorry.* Her words, though you know the truth: *It's okay.*

Your mother can't drive because when all her high school friends were getting permits, she was an undocumented teen with a MetroCard but no ID. She couldn't register for driver education at school, just like she couldn't register for the SATs, the internship program at the job fair, or the state-sponsored writing contests that her English teacher said she should join. She was adopted into the US two years prior, at age fifteen, but her adoption papers weren't finalized by the judge until she had turned seventeen, when she had aged out of her naturalization benefits.

It's not so bad, she thought. *There's the bus and the subway. And New York is a walking city.*

Your mother can't drive because when she tried to learn, she was six months pregnant with you, and it was ninety degrees in her new home state of South Carolina. She told your father that the brake and gas pedals were hard on her swollen ankles and that the Camry's leather upholstery made her sweat. "Too hot, just too hot," she said. But what she didn't say was that sitting in the driver's seat and holding on to the steering wheel made her heart palpitate; that she was sweating not because it was hot out—the AC was set on high—but because her stress hormones were rushing and triggering increased blood flow; that she was sweating because being behind the wheel made her feel like her stomach was on fire and she had to perspire to release the intensity, lest she overheat; and that all she could think of in the moment was *Fight or flight, fight or flight, drive or die. Mama, the road. Mama, there's a car. Mama, they're right behind us. Mama, there's a gun.* She cleared her throat, opened the car door, peeled herself off the leather, and stepped out. Your mother left an imprint of her sweaty back on the seat and her sweaty fingers on the steering wheel. And there, too, she left flashbacks from fifteen years ago.

It's not that bad, she thought. *It'll go away. Must be the hormones. I'll try again when the baby is born.*

Your mother can't drive because when she tried again, you were a newborn who didn't like to sleep. She was tired and sobbed frequently; her crying alternated with yours. She cried in the shower, in the rocking chair, and in bed. She thought it was the isolation—the loneliness that came with early motherhood. So she put you in your car seat, determined to get out of the house that day—to Target, to Walmart, to her friend's house, to any place with people. She carried you in the plastic contraption that was triple your size, but that weighed no less than the dread that clogged her throat and chest. She limped out of the condo, down the hallway, and through the parking lot, the way parents do when they carry around a car seat. But she also limped the way sick and weak people do when suffering from illness, an injury, an accident, or many accidents. She opened the back door on the passenger side of the Camry and maneuvered the car seat onto the base until it locked in place. And as soon as it clicked to latch, you wailed. Your mother shook her head, and said, "No, no, no." She slammed the door shut, ran to the driver side, got in, and buckled up. She put the key in the ignition and turned back once to check on you, only to be reminded that you sat rear facing and with the sun shade shielding you from her sight. You kept wailing. She shifted the gear from park to reverse, stepped lightly on the gas, and lurched, lurched, lurched until the car had pulled out of its parking spot. The go-stop-go-stop quieted you—the tempo of your mother's trepidation lulled you to sleep. "Better," she said, thinking that it was your crying that kept her from operating an everyday machine. She might have even smiled at her reflection in the rearview mirror. But then. As she attempted to hit the gas again, the sweats came, the memories flooded in. She was not with you but back in time, and it wasn't your cries she was hearing, but hers.

At age three, staring at a seven-vehicle scene on the highway: four sedans and two SUVs crushed under a freight truck. At age four, lying across her parents' laps in the back seat, her mother's tears and hair falling on her face, her father singing her awake, her brother saying through tears, "Is she gonna die?" At age nine, riding in her brother's van as he sped away from cops and nearly hit a street vendor. At age ten, living in the same van with her mother because her father had left, her brother, too, and her stepfather had taken over their house and squandered their money. At age eleven, still living in the van with her mother, who had stopped eating and who wept with her forehead on the steering wheel, honking at nothing, honking at the storm that whipped the van from both sides, rocking their metal mobile home with monsoon gusts. At age twelve, hiding under the back seat as her mother flailed a gun in the air. *Shpping! shpping!* the bullets went through the vehicle's metal doors.

Your mother can't drive because she believes everything is her fault. The sedans and SUVs smooshed under the truck was her fault. The head injury was her fault. The car chase was her fault. Living in the van. The crossfire. All her. This is what the trauma specialist, her therapist, has tried to explain to her: "As much as you believe it, it's not true." This is what children of divorced parents, of beaten mothers, of fathers who up and go believe of themselves. This is also what siblings of dead children will spend a majority of their lives unlearning. Mea culpa. Only the monsoon isn't her doing. Only the monsoon she can separate from herself, her intentions, her deeds. The rain gives; the rain takes. She accepts this. But cars are different. Cars are man-made. Cars need operating and therefore, an operator. And she refuses to be the machinist responsible for anything that could hurt you: brown-eyed lover of dolphins, black-haired owner of a canopied princess bed, budding writer of haikus. The rain she'll let you dance in. But cars—cars could take you away from her, like they took away that and that and that and those, too.

Cars are bad, bad, bad. Cars, bad. You, good.

Your mother can't drive, but she is mobile because of words. She's been to many places in her mind because of the books she borrows from the library and the books she buys from the downtown bookstore and the articles your father emails her. She's been to many places in her mind because White was in New England, Didion was in California, Lewis in London, García Márquez in Colombia, Ondaatje in Sri Lanka, Hagedorn in Manila, and Adichie in Nigeria. Her list of authors and places continues to grow; her list of fears shortens. She made a hierarchy of these fears once: at the top was killing someone or dying from a crash and toward the bottom was other motorists giving her the middle finger. She's learned to bike on the road, near cars, at rush hour, and she certainly has been a recipient of the middle finger. She waved and smiled at the giver.

Your mother can't drive, but she reminds herself that she can do difficult things. She went back to school before you turned two, graduated, and wrote part of a book along the way. She took care of you, worked at two cafés, worked at a candle shop, and finished her book before you turned five. By the time you were six, she had a job at your school, two new book ideas, and citizenship papers she had waited fifteen years to get.

Your mother can't drive, but she's stationary for long periods of time, so she's been reading about the frontal lobes, hippocampus, hypothalamus, and thalamus. She's learned so much about trauma, what it does to the brain, what it does to the body, to a child, a mother, a family.

Your mother can't drive, but maybe she can. Last summer she drove a golf cart across a lawn.

Your mother can't drive, but maybe she will, or at least she'll try. *For you, my girl, for you.*

Your mother can't drive, so she walks everywhere, bikes everywhere. She knows where the sidewalk slopes down a little. She tells you about it, and on a snow day, she turns your boogie board into a sled. She knows where the oak trees burst out of the ground and obstruct the road. She tells you about them, and together you write stories about fairies living in trees. She knows the abandoned houses on which the star jasmine crawls. She tells you about them, and on the first day of spring, she takes you there, where the jasmine is in bloom, and she tells you, "They smell as sweet as you."

Your mother can walk anywhere, bike anywhere, but she stays put. She reads to you, teaches you your letters, sings to you. She brushes your hair and braids it into a half ponytail in the mornings, and when she looks in the bathroom mirror to see if the braids are even or if strands are sticking out, she sees you smiling the way she would've smiled at her own mother, had her mother been gentle with her. Your mother kneels down to be at your level, holds your face in her hands, and kisses your nose. She never has to look at you through the rearview mirror because she's looking at you, right in the eye, and she knows, and she knows, and she knows. You are brave.

Why I Write Memoir

I write because I am the last to remember.

I write because my mother lives between personas. She has a condition that she has never sought professional help for, but has been explained by my therapist as dissociative personality disorder. Some days my mother knows she has a daughter and a granddaughter, and I get a text message: What's up? How's the girl? Other days she forgets that I am now married with a child and will reply to my Merry Christmas from us three with Don't forget to moisturize, use pads not tampons, wear a training bra. I don't know where or how she lives; I don't think she does either. Her microamnesias make her days seem like years and her years like days. She forgets to brush her teeth, and she forgets that she has almost died in front of me at least three times.

I write because my father had a stroke in April 2016. Because of it, he experiences cognitive lapses. His diabetes mimics symptoms of Alzheimer's and dementia: he attempts to unlock cars that aren't his, misses medical appointments, scrambles for house keys he's been clutching in his fist all along, and emails the same questions he already asked over voice mail: *How do I copy and paste documents? How do I attach cover letters?* My papa hasn't worked in seven years.

I write because my brother dilutes recollections of broken champagne glasses, knives, and dead babies with vodka, tequila, and beer; he pulverized them along with the pills he crushed to dust and snorted.

He has worked as a club DJ for sixteen years, spinning vinyl for a crowd from nine in the evening until three in the morning and sleeping during the day to evade sunshine and conversation.

I write because even the house we lived in no longer serves us in the business of remembering. It has long been demolished, and where it once was, a minimall now stands. I am as physical as these remembrances get. My mother, father, and brother lead lives of forgetting, while I have made a living out of remembering. My email signature reads: *Cinelle Barnes, Memoirist and Essayist.*

———

I also write to cope with posttraumatic stress, a disorder with manifestations I've experienced since I was thirteen years old: heart palpitations, hypervigilance, overachievement, overexercising, a constant urge to urinate, and the tendency to self-injure. Also, tightness in the throat, difficulty swallowing, difficulty breathing, inability to relax, excessive worrying, nightmares, and flashbacks. Unlike my parents and sibling, I have been blessed with an extraordinary memory in every sense: sensorial memory, explicit memory, implicit memory, episodic memory, and semantic memory.

I remember that my mother's morning tea smelled like tangerines and her perfume like roses and orchids. I remember that my papa's beard felt soft at the chin and coarse by his sideburns; my brother's Teenage Mutant Ninja Turtles were a deep forest green while my father's ferns were sage; our sheets smelled like Clorox and my brother's shirts like baby powder. I remember that blood was crimson on my mother's nightgown and black in her hair. I remember that the dead baby in Mama's arms had two wrinkles on his nose and one chap on his upper lip.

And I remember trying to forget.

When I moved to New York City in my late teens, I stepped off the train at Penn Station thinking, *This is my new life.* The push from commuters through the tunnels and the ascent on the escalator from underground to street level transported me into a new reality, reprogrammed me. For seven years, I partied in the Meatpacking District, went to school in Chelsea, lived and worked on the Upper West and East Sides, brunched in the Lower East, and bought books and clothes and gelato in Williamsburg and DUMBO. I lived at a speed so high, I never had a moment to think, to remember. I went by my childhood nickname. I lost weight and developed defined biceps and abs. I cut my hair. I changed the way I looked, thinking that by doing so, I could change—empty out—my brain.

But then I met a guy. He said, "Tell me everything."

And I did.

He asked me questions like, "If you weren't in art or fashion, what would you be doing?" At the time, I was helping with logistics at a Chelsea gallery and styling photoshoots for an independent fashion magazine. I told him that all I'd ever wanted to do was write.

He gave me a Pilot V5 pen, a lined Moleskine notebook, and a directive: "Go write." I transferred out of fashion school and into a journalism program; I learned how to tell stories. Still, I evaded my own truth. I wrote stories about the tons of waste produced by the fashion industry, infant mortality in Harlem, and sex trafficking in Minnesota. He told me, "You can only avoid your past for so long." He knew where my scars were: upper thigh, inner arm, hippocampus. We dated for nearly four years and got married sixteen months after college graduation. And after just six months of being newlyweds, we unexpectedly got pregnant, and I was overcome by the newness and surprise. I cried as much as I smiled at our baby. Some days I cried more. He told me again, "You can only avoid your past for so long." He gave me a stack of three-by-five index cards, on which he said I should write every time I sat down to nurse the baby.

I wrote everything, and my brain's wiring recircuited to 1986, 1989, 1990, 1993, 1994, 1996, 1997, 1998, 1999, and 2003. The symptoms came back: heart palpitations, hypervigilance, overexercising, a constant urge to urinate, the tendency to self-injure, tightness in the throat, difficulty swallowing, difficulty breathing, inability to relax, excessive worrying, nightmares, and flashbacks.

I told him, "I am breaking."

And he said, "You're becoming you."

Every Thursday at four o'clock, he drove me to therapy. And every Thursday at half past five, he wrapped me in his Marmot jacket, picked me up off the therapist's couch, walked me back to the car, and took me home. He held my hand as he drove through Charleston's sunshowers. He prayed for me. He fed me salsa and chips while I did therapy homework, which was, coincidentally, the same assignment due to my MFA mentor: write your memories; take the ugly and make something beautiful.

The counselor called it *prolonged exposure*, a form of behavioral and cognitive therapy designed to treat PTSD. By re-experiencing the traumatic events through remembering and retelling—in literary terms, (re)creating a sense of time, place, and attitude—I gradually became desensitized from objects and situations that used to cause distress. I went through pictures; followed my mother's paper trail of newspaper clippings, court papers, and health records; and went on a virtual tour of my childhood neighborhood through Google Earth. I interviewed relatives, asking them to describe moments they had witnessed: my parents and the helpers digging a grave in the garden, my mother running and stabbing the air with an envelope opener, and my brother overdosing in his car.

My writing mentors assigned prompts and reading that retrieved data from my brain's long-term and short-term memory banks. I processed the data out loud to my therapist while holding on to tappers— two tappers, one for each hand, that vibrated alternately and stimulated bilateral brain activity: left and right sides, narrative truth and emotional truth, plot and meaning. In other words, *memoir*.

After three years of researching and reliving, two years in an MFA program, and eight months of frequent therapy sessions, I turned in a manuscript of 220 pages to my literary agent. All of my memories, or at least what my body has allowed me to remember, assembled as letters reaching from one side of a page to the other. I can trace them with my fingers, sound them out, and breathe between syllables. I can smooth the pages with the back of my hand, or dog-ear them and slip them into an accordion folder or a file box. I can put them on a shelf, under my desk, or on the bedside table. They are words on a page, just words, and I hold the pen.

I have remembered. And I am new.

———

But did I change my family? Have they also been made new?

My brother and his wife left me messages a few months before my memoir's publication, a long-distance noise barrage from oceans away. They confronted me for digging into our past and accused me of disregarding his state of health and security—they thought that the publication of our childhood story would attract snoopers and harassers. They also accused me of sensationalizing our family history for money, to which I replied, "If I wanted to make money, I'd have taken Papa's advice to go into neurosurgery." But instead of operating on some stranger's brain, I said I was doing the intricate and nimble and low-returns work of authoring a nonfiction book.

"I am writing to get better," I said. "You should try it."

Close to a year after the book was released, my brother's wife messaged to tell me that she and my brother were reading the book together. She said that reading made my brother miss me and that the book brought back good memories—that I wrote *beyond* our trauma, and despite of it. Before this, when my phone would buzz with messages from them and I would see their names under the Facebook notifications list, my heart would stop for a second. I would wait a few days before clicking on the notification banner, if I clicked at all. I tried not to exchange my newfound peace for their cheap thrill of getting to berate me online. And, from my point of view, I withheld interaction as a way to not reward my brother's displaced anger. I know his anger. I know where it comes from. I have told that anger's story. Instead of responding or retaliating, I offered back, somewhere out there, a book with a forest-green and hibiscus-red cover that could mirror to him all the ache that he still carried, all the ache I wish we never had.

My father has listened to and read large sections of the book, but nothing about him has changed. I thought at first that if I organized and presented the details of the past to him, that he might stop running after extrafamilial pursuits and stop running away from the consequences of his choices and his responsibilities to family. I thought that if he learned about what I had to go through after he abandoned us, then he would finally settle down, give up chasing after shiny prospects, and re-create with my daughter whatever safety and closeness I wish he had provided for me when I was her age. But after my father's stroke, and after he received a lump-sum settlement from a company on whose property he fell and broke his arm while in stroke recovery, he withdrew his savings and retirement to invest in a tech start-up.

He has not visited me and my daughter in South Carolina in three years. When I ask him why, he says that he cannot afford a plane ticket. He has placed all his money in his investments and has yet to see returns. I think that part of the aftermath of his stroke is his inability to grasp reality. He claws at illusions of grandeur. Meanwhile, the vinyl flooring in his Queens apartment peels at the corners and rots in certain spots.

Ten months after the book's release, I have learned not to rely on changes in his behavior or beliefs. Doing so is naive and futile to me now. When I stopped expecting my father to change and accepted that writing my version of our story was enough for *my* own sake, I was able to forgive him. But forgiving him did not mean trusting him. Forgiving him did not mean that we had arrived at an agreement, that I did *this* and therefore he must do *that*. Forgiving him did not mean that penitence was paid. Forgiving him did not mean that I now accept his wrongdoings and shortcomings. Forgiving him just meant that I was releasing myself from the chokehold of carrying all the trauma. Acting as family historian, I know now, is really just telling myself the story I already knew. I wait not on anybody else's affirmation, just my own. And here, in expecting only my own validation, is where my freedom lies.

And from my mother, what can I expect? Chaos. I named the book after her, the monsoon, did I not? When my manuscript made it to the legal round of the editing process, which was when my publisher's legal team combed through my sixty thousand or so words, the lawyer had one major concern: my mother might sue me. I was working at a candle shop at the time, making up to four hundred candles per day. I worked on my feet for eight-hour stretches and had signed up to work on both Black Friday and Christmas Eve for the holiday time-and-a-half pay. My daughter had fallen ill the Christmas before when we did not have health insurance. My husband and I took on several part-time jobs to pay off exorbitant student loans and outstanding medical debt. I did not have the energy nor the bandwidth to deal with concerns relating to my mother, whom I had stopped calling after she made comments about my postpregnancy weight and my daughter taking after my darker skin color.

The lawyer asked, "Will you be ready to go against your mother, should she take you to court?"

I said, "Fuck it. I'm fuckin' ready. It's about fuckin' time." I do not curse much, but that day, I did.

While the strategy with my father is to retreat and not act on the offense, the opposite is required when dealing with my mother. I have to be two, even three steps ahead of her if I don't want to fall into any of her traps. When the lawyer warned that my mother—with her cunning ways, her notoriously criminal history, her long record of swindling or bribing people with influence or money—could file a case of defamation against me and the publisher, we put together a list of people who could corroborate my claims and witness in my defense. We changed characters' names and jumbled letters in them until they bore no syllabic nor phonetic resemblance to the real names. I collected newspaper articles and court case summaries, and I audio-recorded testimonies from living relatives, including my father, who said, "No, I wouldn't put it past your mother to come after you."

But perhaps the strongest evidence I have against her is myself. I am not her. I am not a slanderer, a criminal, a negligent parent. When mental health symptoms surfaced for me, I addressed them and sought help. When times were tight, I took on every kind of work, from cleaning houses and doing laundry to answering phones and pouring wax into candle molds. Unlike my mother, I have never conned anyone for money. Instead, I make art. My imagination belongs to me, not I to it. On the other hand, because of her severe and untreated mental illness, my mother's imagination lords over her. She is a slave to the makings of her mind.

But I know who I am. I know where I've been. I can recall. Mama cannot keep track of who she is or who she has been. And is that not my best defense: my sense of control, my ability to decipher? In her splintering into many persons, my mother has not one voice nor one narrative, but a myriad, and no two can substantiate each other. In writing the past, in my remembering, I have made *the* story into *my* story, and I have made room for my one voice.

I am Cinelle Barnes. I have written and I have remembered. And I am well.

My Daughter,
the Future Writer

My seven-year-old daughter wants to become a writer when she grows up. She writes this on an oyster shell with a gold marker and hangs it on a Christmas tree at Marion Square, where she, her classmates, and her teachers have gathered for the annual tree-decorating event. Last year they strung popcorn, and the year before, if I remember correctly, they cut pieces of stale bread into palm-sized stars, lathered them with peanut butter, and rolled them in bird feed. The ornaments of choice have always been edible, at least for the wildlife. This year, the year the city banned the use of plastic straws during tourist season and passed a bill that prohibits single-use bags, and the year we elected an anti-offshore-drilling Democrat to Congress, the school decides to utilize what can be found in any and all waste receptacles in Charleston: oyster shells. The city is known for its oyster bars and oyster roasts. The mollusk is, without exaggeration, everywhere. I once jumped off a boat in Charleston Harbor and landed on a bed of them, cutting my feet in crisscrosses—I was pulled back into the boat by a friend, emerging with what looked like bloodied gills for feet.

Here, we rely on marine life not only for food, but also for attracting tourists, and now the coast is under threat—and actually has been for a long time. Now we are paying attention because the city has had to be evacuated three years in a row due to impending hurricanes and flooding. With each evacuation comes a city-wide shutdown, and with each shutdown, hundreds of thousands of tourist dollars are lost. The tourism industry and rental rates and sea level are rising at equal pace. Our level of care is, too.

So with all this talk about the environment, at home and at school, I think that I am raising a future sustainability expert or an ecologically minded engineer, but no. My daughter pulls me by the hand toward the adorned tree and points at her contribution. "Look, Ma. Read what I wrote."

I want to be a writer when I grow up.

I say, "That's nice." But I know there is nothing nice about being a writer. I hug her anyway and tell her I am proud of her no matter what, and she kisses me hard on my cheek the way my late grandmother used to kiss me—a long, vacuuming sniff. The way Grandma used to kiss me right before she'd tell me that I had overcooked the rice or that I hadn't julienned the carrots thin enough. It is the kiss of Judas. "Like you, Mama. I want to be just like you." I already want to cry. I want to tell her, *Have I not taught you well?!* I smile again and tuck her hair behind her ear, and I take the breath all mothers take when their child has made a declaration that deserves pause ("I kissed someone" or "I am taking a gap year" or "I am dating my boss").

To take my mind off it, I chat my way through the throng of mothers. My girl runs off to play tag with a friend. I ask the moms about the school fund-raiser and the house renovations and the new baby and the new project. I nod and ask follow-up questions. I do and say everything I can to keep the conversation from centering on me. I like to disappear at these things. I have to disappear at these things. When they finally ask me about my writing, I clam up. I zip my jacket all the way up. Then I say the words I've rehearsed in my head: the book that's out is doing well but could get more press, and the book on the way is almost done, but I haven't had time all week to write, not with the teaching and the guest speaking and the online book promoting and the grant writing and constant emailing to ensure I have work coming in the new year and all the other side gigs like calligraphy and office organization I need to take on to afford a life *here* and the electrical fire and the dishwasher leaking, and this, the much-anticipated tree-decorating event. The words come out meandering like an essay and snarky and whiny like a tweet, and not like the gracious, controlled couplet I had imagined it to be in rehearsal. The collective mood falters. Everyone takes a long sip of their latte or tea. I rescue the afternoon and my reputation by saying, "Great idea, these oysters. What have your children written?"

The mothers smile again, thank goodness. Pilot, one says. Ballerina, says another. Scuba diver, painter, veterinarian. "What did your daughter write on hers?"

I tell them she wants to be a writer.

"Oh, like you. How sweet," one says, with the face a person makes when they see a puppy they want to pet. "How special," another says. "Ah, just so special—that they can be anything they want."

"Yes," I say. "I guess."

———

My daughter is in the thick of the first grade bridge unit, the six-week span when her progressive projects-based school encourages curiosity about physical structures such as the bridge. The school does not teach facts nor does it test for a grade. Their job, they believe, is not to fill a child with information. They do not think that a child is an empty vessel waiting to be poured, pounded, or crammed into. Rather, they present concepts that could tease out skills, interests, and propensities innate in the scholar. In the bridge unit, the teachers help the children use all available resources, such as books, the internet, local experts, museums, LEGOs, and their physical surroundings, to investigate what makes a good, sturdy bridge—and how to make it on a small carbon footprint. My daughter comes alive during the unit; it's all she talks about on the way home and at the dinner table. She tells us why the triangle is the most stable shape, and how engineers take into consideration not only the length of the bridge but also the depth at which it will be constructed—Will it be built over a stream or the ocean? As she falls asleep, she mutters the names of the world's longest bridges, oldest bridges, bridges strictly for wildlife use. "There are bridges that can only be used by crabs, Mama." She is a fifth of my age, but I have a fifth of her engineering expertise and physics knowledge. *She might become an engineer, like my father,* I think with much relief.

"Good night, my little engineer," I say.

"No, writer. I'm gonna be a writer." She closes her eyes and that's that. She has my teeth, my cheeks, my hair, and one day, my problems, too.

———

Last October, I sat on my hotel room floor, sobbing. I was in Michigan to record an audiobook, but I was also in the middle of writing a new ten-thousand-word essay while revising an old twelve-thousand-word one. I had also started teaching a series of workshops funded by a museum back home, and I offered language and composition tutoring sessions on weekends. I had agreed to do it all at once because I needed to meet my personal freelance goals and because, as it is in the arts, everything felt like it was now or never—tomorrow nobody might ask about what kind of work I could do for them, how my art could benefit their mission or vision, how my story/ies could fill a void in the cultural conversation they are trying to steer. I was also a working millennial mom, which meant I was as sleepless as new moms, in more debt than older White moms, and I worked like a horse as most people under the age of forty do, but without the luxury of weekends or weeknights or brunch or generational wealth like the latter two often enjoyed. Add to all that the fact that I was Brown, the confusing kind of Brown: Was I Vietnamese? Thai? Latina? Making friends in a predominantly White city was deliberate at best, but more exactly put, it was exhausting because I constantly had to explain who I was, what I was, why I did or didn't do things. And, because I wanted my daughter to be familiar with our Filipino heritage, I took her to events, activities, and restaurants that were thirty to one hundred twenty minutes away from our home.

It took a flight to the Midwest to make me realize how fatigued I was. I was pulled out of the routine I had taught myself to power through, and there, on the pilled Holiday Inn carpet, I curled up into a ball and cried with such desperation my neck veins popped out and my forehead felt fever-hot.

My crying was ugly and loud enough to alert the room service attendant, who slipped a note under my door that said, *Everything okay?* I opened the door and ducked my head out into the hallway, and said, "Hello? You there? Thank you! I'm okay!" I closed the door and headed for the bed, where I hid under the comforter and used the top sheet to wipe my tears as I scrolled for my agent's name on my phone. I called. He answered. "I want to quit," I said. "This is too hard."

He laughed nervously. "We've been through this with book one. This is typical. You're not really quitting."

"No, I really am this time."

He listened to me explain why this is it, why I think I should go back to waiting tables or making candles. Then he said again, "This is typical. You'll go through this again with book three."

There will be no book three, unless it is a children's picture book I can write in a week, I told him. Then I said only sadistic fools made a living writing their most painful memories, that the endless hours and mental rebound and emotional toll were merciless, that my daughter made more money per hour selling lemonade on a street corner. "I don't wish this kind of work on anybody."

He tried the usual response first, told me I was smart and brilliant and that I could make a reader think and feel, that my writing was brave but nonalienating, that my work was timely, resonant. He said we could ask for a deadline extension and a cut on the word count, and I said it didn't matter, I was already beyond my threshold. I had run out of whatever it took to produce material that someone would not only want to read but also pay for. He said I was a bottomless well of stories, and I rolled my eyes and grumbled. When he felt like the agent-y answers weren't having an effect except maybe pissing me off, he finally said, "Hey, I'm having a hard week, too, if that makes you feel any better." The rest of our talk then became about how excruciating the publishing industry was, how much we gave for the little we got. I asked him if he had been excited by a pitch or manuscript that had landed on his desk recently, and, with a sudden change in tone and energy, he told me about a novel, a work of investigative nonfiction, a memoir, a middle-grade book, and a book of literary criticism. He said he was going to Nebraska for a university-sponsored literary event, something he looked forward to each year. He blathered on about prospects and projects, and I put him on speaker phone. I unfurled from the braid of sheets I had wound around me in my writhing and sat up on the side of the bed as he continued to rave about his clients. He truly was proud of every one of us.

My phone started to buzz—a FaceTime call from my husband was coming in.

"Hey, hate to stop you, but I'm getting a call from home," I said.

"Oh, yeah, of course. Take it. I'll email you once I've renegotiated, okay?"

"Okay. Thank you."

"Hang in there. Don't quit."

———

"Mama, when can I read your book?"

My daughter is referring to *Monsoon Mansion*, the book I began writing when she was born, the book that took six years to write, revise, and publish, the book that I basically raised alongside her. It is almost like a sibling to her. It shares physical space in her room—a row of hardcovers on the top shelf in front of her bed, and a box of paperbacks on the floor. When the book was still an accordion folder of drafts, it lived on an IKEA desk in the corner of the nursery, where I could be far enough away from the dishes, laundry, television, and—where I promised myself it would never interfere—the marital bed. As the book was being printed and bound, distributed and displayed, my daughter was learning phonetic sounds, silent letters, and some of the most commonly used words in the English language: *I, am, is, are, the, want, to, be, a*.

When we launched the book at the Charleston Library Society, my daughter wore her favorite purple sequined dress and greeted guests at the door. From there, I toured to places as near as Charlotte and as far as Oakland, with my daughter in the plane seat next to me and copies of the book and some autograph pens in the carry-on under the seat before me. At book signings, she sat on my lap and finished off my signature with a heart in glittery pink ink. The book's epilogue, which I like to read from at these events, ends with a scene where she's diving into a pool: "And she is shining, sparkling, gliding underneath the hot sun . . . She has touched the dark waters ebbing from my past. With light. Of light." She has heard me read these last lines out loud to different crowds, but she does not know the chapters that come before, what I was writing all along as she napped in her crib or in my arms.

"Mama, I said, when can I read your book?" When she is adamant about something, she juts her jaw slightly to the right so her upper front teeth do not line up with the bottom ones.

"You look like Popeye when you do that," I say, digressing.

"Who is Popeye? And tell me when I can read it!"

I tell her who Popeye is and that she should wait until she is ready to read longer works. I remind her that the longest book she's read is thirty-two pages, with pictures. I commend her on how hard she's worked on her reading this year. "Soon you'll get to fifty pages, then seventy-five, then the two hundreds. Then you'll be ready for mine!"

"It's nonfiction, right?" she asks, having just learned the difference between the genres. "It means it all happened in real life. You didn't just imagine it."

"Yes," I say. And I think of why I wrote the book in the first place—to learn whether or not the images in my head were imagined, whether or not they happened, whether or not they happened to me.

"I'll write about *my* real life one day," she says, plunging her fork into her bowl of pasta.

I make a suggestion to write about fairies, the ballet, mongooses, talking cats, or even bridges to neverlands. "You *loved* learning about bridges. You were so sad when the bridge unit ended. Maybe you can write something about them?"

"Maybe, Ma." She scoots off her chair and walks to our roller cart of art supplies for a pen and paper. She sits back down, shoves a forkful of pasta into her mouth, folds the paper lengthwise, and writes on the front: *About Me.*

———

My husband is away for work and will not be back for a few more days. My daughter has planted herself in our bed, which I like because I'm the restless, lonely sleeper type. It is why I cannot sleep at hotels and likely why I end up crying at some point when I am away, overtired and vulnerable. The dog, who is typically not allowed on our soft furnishings, has also been sleeping on the bed. He loves it so much, I have to carry him out the door for his last quick walk for the night. Comfortable now that I am surrounded by breathing beings, whose limbs all fall on some part of me, I fight sleep as it comes prematurely. Asleep before 9:00 p.m. means I'll be up before 4:00 a.m., the worst time to be awake when you're a nonfiction writer prone to anxiety and flashbacks.

I slide from underneath my daughter and dog and pull myself toward the little light above the stove. It shines just enough soft yellow across the kitchen counter and on one side of the dining table, and right where it ends, my daughter's "book" rests. I sit down by it and trace the letters of the title with my finger, and I consider opening it but feel like I am prying. It's hard enough to ensure the anonymity and privacy of family when you make a living writing about your own life. How much more intrusion can my daughter withstand? I think of that idea some more, how here, in her sleep, she has dreams I might never know about, and that's a gift. She has pages she wants to fill, a rendition of the story that will not be mine nor ours, but just hers. I think of how much exposure she's had to the literary world, not only from having spent the majority of a year on the road with me and meeting editors and writers I swooned after for years, but also from climbing on my desk chair as I typed on the computer. I swatted her quick hands away from the keyboard as she tried to type *jxbdteygcvjnpoigfhgmshl!* into one of my chapters. At the playground, when she had found a friend, I dashed from the sandbox to the bench where my manuscript and red editing pen waited. When she was even smaller and still nursed, I wrote on index cards or spoke into my phone's recorder as she suckled. I have clearly made the impression that there is something so captivating and marvelous about words that I made them my company, sometimes my sole company, through early motherhood. Why would she not want to try it, too? Her school believes that we introduce concepts to tease out what is already within. Here's the tease; now what is within?

Is it because she was born in the Lowcountry of South Carolina, where centuries-old oaks bowed down over the road when we brought her home for the first time? Or the cypress knees that she sees sprout

out of the marsh and the egrets that perch on them? The oysters? We have fragrant jasmine, too, and magnolia thick with their recognizable leaves and history and memories.

Or in there, in the hippocampus and the amygdala, which she recently learned the functions of at her progressive school, do less idyllic scenes reoccur? There was her birth, when everyone held their breath waiting to see who she would look like. My family hoped she'd have her father's green eyes or at the very least hazel, and that she'd have skin that was fairer than mine. Filipinos love their light-skinned children. What a letdown it was for them, I remember, when I flew her to New York to meet family when she was not even two months old. They did say she was beautiful. But they also said, disappointedly, that her eyes were dark, her nose was small, and that she was not born with the one supposedly good thing Asian babies are born with: a full head of thick, black hair. My baby had a halo of wisps, and it was exactly that: a feathery ring of brown around the crown of her head but none on top. I whispered so many prayers when they expressed dissatisfaction, hoping that she'd be protected from the damaging, White-aspiring, self-erasing, poisonous, postcolonial beliefs held by my family. I protected my baby, and myself, by seeing family infrequently and cloistering us in Southern living, a way of life that had been presented to me in maga-zines and other media as hospitable, comfortable, and at the time of my pregnancy, Instagram-worthy country-chic.

My mother-in-law, ever gentle and genteel, became my source of comfort and safety. She prepared calorie-heavy casseroles so I could replenish my body after nursing and produce more breastmilk. She taught me how to put baby mittens on, how to correctly and swiftly wipe and diaper a newborn, and how to hold an infant with her belly flat on my forearm so I could burp her, shush her, and cook at the same time. My mother-in-law also drove me around so that my hus-band's relatives could meet the baby. And that was when another kind of seemingly harmless yet psychologically damaging dialogue began to surround us. They said my baby was so pretty because she was, in their words, half Filipino, which made her *interesting* or worse, *exotic*. The comment might have seemed like a compliment to my people and heritage at first, but I had repeatedly, almost routinely, received the same message from Americans since arriving here as a teenager. I know the subtext. When people say things like "Filipinas are beautiful" or "Filipinas are meant for beauty pageants" or "You're beautiful because you're . . . ," what they are really saying, though they might not be conscious of it, is that we are useful in this certain way—in the way that unicorns, mermaids, and fairies are useful for fantastical lore. They sexualize and mythologize our existence so that fantasies and myth are where we exist—and only there. For as long as we are beautiful and magical and enchanted in these otherworldly, sexualized ways, we will remain outside their circles, their families, their spheres of comfort and familiarity. Para-normal, or outside of the norm. In other words, other.

Will it be these stories of otherness that will fill my daughter's book? Will she write about the time a little blonde girl touched her elbow and asked, "Why are you Brown?" I was standing by the door, picking her up from a playdate, when the question was asked. My daughter, then six, thought for a minute and said, "Because my mama is Brown." Then she looked at me and smiled, proud of her cleverness. I smiled back, but I didn't want to have to. I didn't want to have to affirm my daughter's quick wit and thinking on her feet because soon enough, it will become repetitive, exhausting. She will have to come up with such responses to explain or excuse herself over and over again, while the other party will get away with being "innocent." That was what the girl's mother said, after all, that it was an innocent comment. I do believe that children are innocent, but situations and stations are not. Every time something is made to pass as innocent, I ball a little fist inside my sweatshirt pocket because people keep giving other people's children passes for their innocence, while they keep robbing my daughter of hers. When someone touches my daughter's elbow or upper arm or hair, something is broken into and broken inside her. While I agree that children say the silliest, most unintentionally hurtful things, I do think that it is up to these children's parents and their communities to teach them more honestly and comprehensively, to bring them in closer proximity to things that, to them, are distant and unfamiliar now but that can become frightening or alarming or worth calling the cops for later. I read a line from Glennon Doyle Melton's blog once: "Fear can't survive proximity."

Where we live, my daughter is often the only proximity these other children have to Brownness, to Asianness, to her certain kind of otherness. I know many of them don't want it to be so, but intention is never the point. Even snails have intention. Some scientists say even plants do, too. Action is what my daughter and I await and need.

My daughter and I, like these other families, can also opt for inaction, or antiaction, and hide behind our no-accent accents, behind the impression of celebrity and intelligence that my occupation gives off, or behind the fact that the other head of our household is a Southern, White male with multiple degrees. We can armor ourselves with our different rudiments of passability, from my knowledge of the English canon to the Scandinavian DIY feel of our home's interior, or even our Christian roots, and misuse the sense of agency with which we either prop up other people of color, or step on them to get ahead or merely stay alive. Being Filipino can mean that we are in the in-between of White and Black/Latinx. This is what scholars such as Elaine H. Kim have called *racial triangulation*, or the reality described as the Asian/ Asian American having to choose between supporting Whiteness or unhooking from it.

In our life, it plays out as spending Saturdays at the mall that White families from my daughter's school do not visit. At the mall, she jumps and climbs in the play area where five out of six children are of color. On Sundays, it means driving thirty to forty minutes north of where we live so we can go to a church with Spanish speakers, Asian congregants, and a pastor who is not only African American but also native to Charleston. Habitually and unprompted, my daughter says as she steps out of the car, "I like our new church. I like that I'm not the only Brown kid here." I stay in the car for a few more seconds when she says this, locking in with me the air in which she spoke these words, sitting in it to let it marinate: My daughter says she is happy; what a relief. But she says she is happy *here*. How does she feel elsewhere?

After Sunday supper at the church hall, we drive another twenty minutes to the naval base so my daughter can participate in traditional Filipino dance and eat a merienda of pancit and ube ice cream from the commissary. When Monday rolls around, we are a little deprived of our culture and language, so we watch YouTube videos of Ruby Ibarra and Rivermaya.

When the Asia unit begins at the school, I volunteer time for a show-and-tell that includes not felt cutouts nor Google printouts, but hand-embroidered Philippine slippers, handwoven Philippine bags and fans, and cups of coconut water and mango juice imported from back home. I bring a stack of books that have Filipino protagonists or authors, and I tell the students a short anecdote about my life as a child. I tell them that hearing and sharing personal narrative is much more accurate, authentic, and inclusive than learning about a people through Wikipedia, the encyclopedia, or *National Geographic*. While I am not the first Asian or Asian American parent to volunteer time in this way for the school, I am the first Filipino one. I offer to do it to give my country and daughter representation, and to see to it that the students understand that Asia is large and populous and diverse in culture, history, religion, and politics—that we are not all the same.

Most importantly, I do it for my girl. I do it so she feels mirrored when she sits crisscross-applesauce on the foam mat. I do it so she feels like she can do it, too.

At a school function, I ask another mother if she wants to raise funds for scholarships for students of color. I say, "Since our children go to a progressive school, don't you think it's worth asking who we are progressing?" She, who moved from New York and has the aspirations of someone who has lived in an international city, asks how we can get more children of color to receive the top-notch education our children get. I say that taking reparations and equity advancement seriously means more than just supplying the school library with "diverse" books, that it would take people like her writing numerous letters and making incessant calls to raise and allocate funds for students of color and their families—that the advancement committee would not only need to garner monetary support for tuition and fees for students of color, but also for their backpacks, uniforms, lunches, transportation, and the dollar equivalent of hours their parents or guardians will spend helping with homework or attending school events, and the dollar equivalent of the work hours lost when the school is on break or holiday and childcare is necessary.

When I help with after-school care, I walk to where the Mexican cleaning lady's grandchildren are playing with vacuum cleaner attachments and ask if they want to play with the students. I call them by their names, just like I do with the matriculated kids, and I urge them to correct their new friends when their names are mispronounced. "CARlos, not Cahr-lowes."

When Friday arrives, my husband is beat from a week of work, and I am, too. But I am also tired from responding to Instagram messages from readers and online trolls—questions like, *How can we make our local moms group more sensitive to the needs of children of color?* or *Do you feel like you post too much about, or go to too many, Filipino things?* In late October, after my meltdown at the hotel, I do myself and my family a favor: I quit social media. When Thanksgiving comes around, I host a Friendsgiving at our place and invite only immigrant families. I serve them ensaymada, and I don't have to explain what it is. I actually have a good, restorative holiday. I eat my sweet roll and even dunk it in my coffee. I chase it with a prawn cracker steeped in chili vinegar, and nobody winces.

To live freely—does it not mean not having to explain? Then why, after all the freedom I have tried to afford her, does my daughter want to become a writer? Why does she want to spend a lifetime telling people who, what, when, where, why, and how? Why does she want to expend her energy elucidating, illuminating, enumerating, justifying the existence of . . . all that she is? She can just be.

She can just be an engineer.

Engineers busy themselves with what is: A equals B, or this here is the cause of that effect there. This is this, that is that. Nobody questions, nobody messages on Instagram, nobody trolls, nobody stops her midmeal to ask what her opinion is on what is more important: racial unity or the environment? It is exhausting enough to be Brown in Whitelandia. For her sake, I hope my daughter chooses a career that will not leave her pried open for people who will salivate just to see her bleed.

But I am being dramatic. Part of the job, too, no?

Physics. I hope my girl studies physics.

———

I am almost out of activities the night before my husband returns from his work trip, so my daughter reminds me that she received an interactive world map on her birthday. We retrieve it from her pile of year-end hoarding. I open the packaging with my teeth, pull out the meter-wide glossy sheet, and try to read the instructions printed on the wrapper I had just ripped in half. Stickers fall out as my daughter unfolds the map, and we begin to understand what the interactive aspect of the map is all about: stickers of penguins, koalas, the Statue of Liberty, etc. are to go on their respective parts of the world. My daughter peels off a Matryoshka doll sticker and asks where it goes. I point at Russia. She does the same for a yeti, a baguette, a basket of pineapples and macadamia, and so on. I tell her where they all go. "Mom, how do you know all this?" she asks with big eyes.

I tell her I've always been a collector of information. "You learn a little about everything from being a writer."

She gasps and follows it by saying, "You can be anything!"

I don't know what she means, but I don't ask. I keep stickering, placing landmarks and indigenous wildlife and plants where they belong. She keeps gasping and says, ". . . and find Amazon birds . . . and climb the Great Wall . . . and cross the London Bridge . . . and train capuchin monkeys . . ." We finish marking the map, but her gleeful waffling does not end. She jumps onto her bed and bounces. "Anything! Anything!" she shouts. "Monday, a scientist! Tuesday, a pilot! Wednesday, an artist! Thursday, Mary Poppins!"

She jumps and exclaims this nonsense she is proud of for several minutes more, then she plops on top of her sheets like a splat of slime. I splat out next to her, bulldozer over her legs, and say, "Friday, a construction worker paving a road!" When I am on the other side, she plows right back over me, and we go back and forth, turning it into a game.

"Time-out, Mama," she says, making a T with her hands. "I'm tired."

"Okay," I say, and I brush her hair away from her face and study the beads of sweat forming on her nose. I blow them off. I kiss where they were. I thank God for time alone with her, and I think to myself that this should be the only way, and reason, she should ever tire.

The following essays originally appeared in other publications. All have been edited and revised for this collection.

"Why Your Mother Can't Drive" in BuzzFeed.

"The Gulf Between, the War Within" originally published as "How a War in the Middle East Changed My Family in the Philippines Forever" in *Catapult*.

"Carefree White Girls, Careful Brown Girls" first appeared in *Catapult* and was published in its original version.

"Why I Write Memoir" first appeared in *South 85 Journal*.

Acknowledgments

Many thanks to my husband, daughter, and dog. On particularly trying days, I see them as a hindrance to my work and art, and yet I remember that they are my reason and my fuel. They are my soft place to land. I thank them for bearing with the mood swings that come with the deadlines, and the house that is never (will never be) clean. (This is a thank-you, not an apology.) I thank them for allowing me to write about our life/lives (again), and I promise to write about something else the minute they ask me to. Thank you, you three, for always being there for me. I love you and thank God for you.

Also always there for me are Vivian Lee, my editor, and Noah Ballard, my agent.

Vivian has taught me so much and has supported me through so much. She goes above and beyond what editors do for their writers, and I really don't know how to maintain a professional relationship with her—I just want to hug her all the time. Particularly for this book, she *freed* me from certain lies and insecurities I had about being a writer, a woman, and a person of color, and she has lent me her ear and eyes multiple times. She has shown me how to courageously and healthily navigate the publishing system and has pushed me to write more honestly and comprehensively these past couple of years.

Noah continues to trust me and my ideas, and also trust that I can handle rejection, negotiation, and rebuttal. He believes that my work is important, probably more than I do at times. He listens. I thank him for always having been friendly, easy to talk and vent to, but quick and stern when necessary. And, of course, for making sure I have projects that pay—writers gotta eat and get their teeth cleaned, too.

Much gratitude goes out to friends and family everywhere, especially my BFFs who are always only a text away. Their support, prayers, care packages, Venmo surprises, text messages, and visits make life easier. Thank you to friends Stefani, Ceara, and Jasmine, cousin Ashley, and my husband's parents for keeping my daughter after school and on weekends—they made the writing of this book possible. Thanks as well to everyone at Citadel Mall for allowing me to use the food court and play area as my office. Parent-artists, we can do this.

My thanks to my writing teachers who taught me what it meant to *assayer*: Jim Minick, Susan Tekulve, Richard Tillinghast, Elmaz Abinader, Harry Bruinius, Hua Hsu, Ava Chin, and Robert Olmstead.

So much love to readers, bookstagrammers, and booksellers everywhere. I write for me, but I write for you, too.

Thank you to the Halsey Institute of Contemporary Art, VONA, Kundiman, and the Converse College MFA program. Your collective work makes art possible and sustainable, and your recognition of my work has encouraged me and pushed me forth. All my gratitude goes out to my VONA Political Content workshop group for their love, support, and valuable feedback.

My thanks to the editors of the published essays here: Jarry Lee at BuzzFeed, Megha Majumdar and Matt Ortile at *Catapult*, and Debby DeRosa and Kristi Hébert at *South 85 Journal*, and the amazing teams at Little A. Thanks to Hafizah Geter for adopting this project and running it to the finish line. Also to writers whose books guided the writing of this one: Alexander Chee, Kiese Laymon, Nicole Chung, M. Evelina Galang, Gina Apostol, Elaine Castillo, Crystal Wilkinson, Kristal A. Sital, Zeyn Joukhadar, Devi Laskar, and Hala Alyan.

Maraming salamat to Monica Ramos for giving this book her art. To Ruby Ibarra for creating music that put a fire in me and got me started on this project.

Thank you to Filipinos who venture far to provide for their families and our nation. Lupang hinirang, duyan ka ng magiting. Sa manlulupig, 'di ka pasisiil. May you return home to the land of the morning—sa duyan ng magiting. And may your sacrifices not go unnoticed.

Thank you to anyone who has ever extended grace and generosity to immigrants and the displaced. I pray peace, joy, and strength over each of you.

About the Author

Photo © Joshua Garcia

Cinelle Barnes is a memoirist, essayist, and educator from Manila, Philippines. She is the author of *Monsoon Mansion: A Memoir*, which was listed as a Best Nonfiction Book of 2018 by *Bustle* and nominated for the 2018 Reading Women Nonfiction Award. She is also the editor of a forthcoming anthology of essays about the American South by writers of color. Having earned an MFA degree in creative nonfiction from Converse College, Cinelle has written for BuzzFeed, *Catapult, Literary Hub, Hyphen, Panorama: The Journal of Intelligent Travel*, and *South 85 Journal*, among others. Her work has received fellowships and grants from VONA, Kundiman, the National Endowment for the Arts, the North Charleston Arts Fest, and the Lowcountry Quarterly Arts Grant. Barnes was the 2018–19 writer-in-residence at the Halsey Institute of Contemporary Art in Charleston, South Carolina, where she and her family live. For more information, visit www.cinellebarnes.com.